PAISLEY
PUBLIC LIBRA ...NG

Central Library, High
Telephone: PAisley 2360

Thursd.. .....y
10 a.m. — 8 p.m.

Wednesday and Saturaay
10 a.m. — 5 p.m.

MSC.

or author

or class!

NOT TO BE W/D
S.U.C.

30/6/86

FINES:—Fines for detention
will be charged according to
the bye-laws.

RENEWALS:—Period of loan
may be renewed if the book
is not required by another
borrower.

**BOOKS DAMAGED OR
LOST:**—Readers are required
to take care of books issued
to them. Loss or damage
must be made good and the
value of books lost or
damaged will be charged.

This book is due for return
on latest date stamped on
card.

**PLEASE DO NOT REMOVE
CARD**—6d. fine will be
charged if lost.

ALL THE PAINTINGS OF
TITIAN

Part 1
VOLUME TWENTY-NINE
in the
Complete Library of World Art

The Complete Library of World Art

ALL THE PAINTINGS

OF TITIAN

Part 1 (1488–1545)

Text by FRANCESCO VALCANOVER

Translated from the Italian by
SYLVIA J. TOMALIN

OLDBOURNE
London

© 1965 by Rizzoli Editore, Milan
Published in Great Britain by
Oldbourne Press, 1–5 Portpool Lane,
London E.C.1

Printed and bound in Great Britain by
Jarrold & Sons Ltd, Norwich

CONTENTS

ALL THE PAINTINGS OF
TITIAN

TITIAN

Life and Work

WE have no precise information on Titian's early years. He was born in Pieve di Cadore about 1488 —a more probable date than the traditional one of 1477. His family had for some time been highly regarded in their mountain village, because of their wealth and civic standing. Tradition, today upheld by Ridolfi, has it that as a boy Titian already showed an inclination towards painting. He is said to have painted a *Madonna* "on a book-heading using the juice of flowers as colors." According to legend, too, he served his apprenticeship in his native district under Antonio Rosso, an unassuming late-comer to Bartolomeo Vivarini's and Gian Francesco da Tolmezzo's circle.

The scant information given by Dolce on the period before Titian's sudden appearance, together with Giorgione, at the Fondaco dei Tedeschi in 1508 is consequently all the more valuable.

Titian's intuitive choice of masters from the Venetian artistic milieu, which was full of colorful personalities at that time, is already evident in the famous passage in Dolce's *Dialogo dell'Aretino*, possibly suggested by the artist himself. The wide vistas of his native valley still with him, the young man from Cadore developed rapidly as an artist when he found himself suddenly plunged into the fascinating kaleidoscope of life in the lagoon city, then at its zenith of splendor. He first frequented the workshop of Sebastiano Zuccato, and absorbed the chromatic splendor of the mosaics in the Basilica of San Marco. Then he went on to the more famous workshop of Gentile Bellini, the most highly regarded of the Venetian "ceremonial painters." While Titian admired the vast, clearly constructed narrative painting of Gentile, he must also have noted the static medieval nature of his style, and was more attracted to the work of Gentile's brother Giovanni, with more fruitful results.

All the fundamental artistic developments of the second half of the fifteenth century, from Donatello to Mantegna, from Piero della Francesca to Antonello da Messina, were summarized in Giovanni Bellini's paintings. Titian was fascinated by the humane tenderness of Giovanni's idealized sacred figures, which transmuted Piero della Francesca's impassiveness and Antonello's abstract idealism. Bellini presented his figures with an iconographic monumentality and formal architectural severity that stemmed from the sinuous quality of his line and from the dissolving of the numerous relationships between chromatic values. It was only in his last years, after the *San Zaccaria Altarpiece* of 1505, that Bellini partly overcame this dependence on the precepts of drawing and perspective by use of a new tonal translucence. This was a result of the influence of the "modern style" fostered by Giorgione in the first years of the century.

It is therefore no surprise to find Titian, whose contact with Bellini had revealed fifty years of Venetian painting to him, approaching Giorgione to learn how to "paint only the colors themselves, without further drawing studies on paper" (Vasari). Giorgione only attained complete expression by means of color about 1505, following earlier hesitant attempts in the Castelfranco altarpiece. The human figure lost its fifteenth-century "heroic" outline in the full, independent use of the laws of linear perspective, and in the transparency of the colors used, with their unlimited luminous shadings. Thus the human figure became an integral part of nature in a realistic conception of space, modified though this was. It was a new and more intimate world of subtle rhythm, sensual Pan-like naturalism; and Giorgione was able to give form to his lyrical melancholic dreams set in the framework of contemporary cultural life of Venice (open as it then was to the influences of Neoplatonist philosophy and the Arcadian idyll).

It has been rightly assumed that the young Titian was so fascinated by his master's use of color and tried so hard to imitate him, that "sometimes his pictures were mistaken for works by Giorgione" (Vasari). Soon, too, Titian was following Giorgione's example in society and culture and became accepted by the new intellectual *élite* of Venetian aristocracy.

Even while fascinated by Giorgione, Titian showed early signs of precocity. There is clear evidence of this both in the writings of his contemporaries and (even more valuable) in his own first documented works: the frescoes of the Fondaco dei Tedeschi, and of the Scuola del Santo in Padua.

Titian worked on the frescoes of the Fondaco dei Tedeschi in 1508 as an independent collaborator, but subordinate to Giorgione. This is evident from both the absence of his name from the official documents of the time and by the allocation of labor: the decoration of the façade facing the Grand Canal was given to the older and established master; the walls facing the Ponte di Rialto and Merceria where the decoration would be hardly visible among the narrow lanes were assigned to the younger artist. By the eighteenth century the frescoes were already damaged by salt, and today all that remains are two almost indecipherable fragments.

However, Piccini's prints (Part 4, plate 186a) and Zanetti's (Part 4, plates 186b and 187), although imprecise indicate that Titian's admiration for Giorgione was none the less mixed with independence from the older master.

The paintings of both Giorgione and Titian are characterized by a monumentally scaled interpretation of the human figure, and already show the new classicism imposed on Rome and Florence by Michelangelo and Raphael (possibly brought to Venice by Fra Bartolommeo, who was there in 1508). Although Giorgione's nudes surprise one in the way in which their grand proportions are isolated in his architectonic conception of space, they still form part of the restrained purity of construction to be found in the dream-like transparency of the *Three Philosophers* (Vienna) and the *Venus* (Dresden). On the other hand, Titian's figures, pulsating with a very earthy humanity, have quite a different vitality: they almost force themselves into space with their easy, free poses, and daring foreshortening. They suggest new, expressive possibilities of color and light and shade.

Although today it is difficult to agree with Dolce that Titian was "superior to his master" in the Fondaco dei Tedeschi frescoes, certainly his independent personality established itself three years later in the fresco cycle *The Miracles of St Anthony* (plates 23, 26 and 30) in the Scuola del Santo in Padua. The break with three different currents is basic and far-reaching: not only with the heroic world of Giovanni Bellini which had been evoked with religious fervor in an intermingling of form and color, or with the brightly colored tales told by Carpaccio in his spatial perspectives; but also with the lyrical, dream-like and sensuous human figures Giorgione depicted.

Titian opposes all this with a firm grasp of reality: man triumphs with all the force of his feelings and passions. No longer isolated in lonely enchantment, man is dialectically alive and fully participant.

On the walls of the Scuola del Santo, Titian was not required to portray (as in the Fondaco dei Tedeschi) abstruse allegories understandable only to a select circle. He had to represent various popular miracles of St Anthony for the edification of pious friars and the people. Devoid of any iconographic or literary overtones, these scenes make an immediate impression on the spectator by the straightforwardness with which the figures are portrayed.

In the *Miracle of the Youth's Leg* (plate 26) the saint in the center stretches out his hand with a sure, firm gesture towards the young man who is supported by his pleading mother. In a large semicircle round them are the solemn-faced spectators: some are sceptical, some truly believing, others merely curious. Behind them, the landscape rises to a luminous sky, intersected by a great tree.

In *St Anthony Healing a Newborn Child* (plate 23), the culminating point of the miracle is portrayed. The psychological center of the action is the child—who forgives his mother, outlined against the gray tunic of the saint—the hinge of the composition. Participants and spectators encircle the scene. The unjust accuser—the husband and father —gazes with lowered eyes at the newborn child speaking in defense of his mother's virtue. She appears in profile, a dignified and reserved figure. To the left, the composition is marked by movement and excitement (plate 24): a young man suddenly turns his head, and seems to be urging his friends to hurry to see the miracle. Beside him is another handsome youth, his silver cloak flaring about him, forming a vivid mosaic of color with the green of his shirt and the red and yellow of his stockings.

The dramatic momentum created by the narrative and

13

rhythmic groups of figures is echoed in the background, with its contrast between the dark mass of the building (broken by the luminous whiteness of the mutilated statue representing a Roman emperor) and the pale sky lit by a red glow, against which the hillside stands out in silhouette.

The third scene, the *Jealous Husband* (plate 30), centers on the cruel episode itself. In the background we catch a glimpse of the husband kneeling before the Miracle Worker and begging him to save his wife's life. The dynamic contrast of light and shade, and the violence of the gestures blocked out against a rocky, wind-blown precipice, the dramatic fury of the homicide and the convulsive terror of the woman thrown to the ground—all are treated with a hitherto unheard-of boldness (plate 31). Just as persuasive a proof of its greatness is found in the preparatory sketch in Paris (see illustration with comment on page 52).

The three miracles of the saint are thus linked by vivid human feeling, and it seems almost as though they take place amid everyday scenes—in which, however, the episodes are transposed to an idealized plane, without ever being colored by rhetoric, let alone by forced melodrama. The human figures dominate the scenes in easy rhythmic relationships and in a simple and natural extension of forms. But on looking closer, we see that in fact they are all executed with sure logic. The function of color is the determining factor in this exaltation of life. Giorgione, shading his tones in a translucent atmosphere, attenuated the values of the tonality, giving cohesive form to his lyric vision. Titian, on the other hand, concentrates on harmonic and simplified contrasts of extensive planes of color, which in their overwhelming simplicity stand out luminously as dynamic contrasts of light and shade. In these scenes—more vital and intense even than reality, where man and nature are celebrated in a chorus of dazzling beauty, truly classical in its idealism—an artist of little over twenty, a product of the High Renaissance no less than Michelangelo and Raphael, reveals himself.

The woodcut depicting the *Triumph of Faith* (see pages 56–57) is recorded by Vasari as having been executed in 1508, but Ridolfi connects it with a frieze painted by the artist "around the walls of a room in a house taken by him" in Padua during the time that he was working on the frescoes in the Scuola del Santo. The woodcut probably dates from Titian's Padua period. It shows a long procession of figures from the Old and New Testaments together with monks and virgins singing the praises of Christ. Christ is seated on a cart pushed by the four Church Fathers and drawn by the symbols of the Evangelists. Although perhaps inspired by Savonarola's description of the *Triumph of Christ*, the model for this print is none the less Mantegna's *Triumphs of Caesar* (now at Hampton Court). It is, therefore, of the greatest interest in that it tells us how, from the very first, Titian was driven by his experiments in form (which were opposed to Venetian tradition) to avoid the dreamy qualities of Giorgione. Even more significant is the way in which the artist dominates and transforms everything he borrows, so that his forms pulsate with tremendous life and vitality. To see an instance of this we need only look at the *Miracles of St Anthony* (plates 23–31).

We know of no other documented works from the years during which Titian was executing the Fondaco dei Tedeschi and Padua frescoes. However, a group of paintings at one time attributed mostly to Giorgione and still under discussion today can be assigned to Titian because of their difference, in varying degrees, from Giorgione's last works and their evident stylistic and spiritual affinities with the Padua frescoes.

Among the earliest of these is the *Lucretia* (plate 1), formerly in the Fleishmann Collection and the Goldmann *Portrait of a Man* (plate 2). In their simplified and immediate presentation (plate 3), they seem as near to some of Titian's Fondaco dei Tedeschi figures as they are distant from Giorgione's.

The *Birth of Adonis* (plate 4a), the *Forest of Polydorus* (plate 4b) in the Museo Civico in Padua, and the *Orpheus and Eurydice* in the Accademia Carrara, Bergamo (plate 8) belong more to Giorgione's world, although the *Orpheus* may be a later work. They are examples of the pastoral "poetry" so greatly admired by contemporaries and of which Paolo Pino wrote enthusiastically in 1548: "I have seen miraculous landscapes by the hand of Titian which are more graceful than the Flemings' ever were." But even though the *Tempest* may have directly inspired Titian's smaller works, Giorgione's lyrical landscape is transformed: nature is more spacious, more dynamic, orchestrated cleanly in chromatic planes against which small human figures stand out vividly. They are both inventive and colorful in an atmosphere of clear light.

Titian did not, however, forget Bellini. The painting commemorating the victory of the papal and Venetian fleets over the Turks in 1502 (plate 10) was long thought to be Titian's earliest documented work, executed at the time of the battle or shortly afterwards, and the result of a renewed interest in Bellini. The composition of the picture, especially the figure of St Peter (plate 12), is so close to Giovanni Bellini that it would seem to have been executed at the beginning of the century. However, one look at the energetic form and emotional content of the figures achieved by dense and luminous rich color convinces us that the canvas is closer to, if not later than, the Padua frescoes. Moreover—

and Suida was the first to point this out—the fluidity of pictorial expression with which the mock relief (plate 11) and the marine background are portrayed lead us to believe that the picture may have been taken up again and finished towards the end of the second decade.

Titian's capacity for renewing traditional iconographic subjects in a new and highly personal manner appears in other youthful works: small devotional paintings such as the Bache *Madonna* (plate 13), who is portrayed in an affectionate exchange with the Child against an open landscape bordered on the left by a curtain; the New Haven *Circumcision* (plate 14), still intensely expressive in its vividly natural composition despite color deterioration. Also in this category is the Duveen *Portrait of a Woman* (plate 19), whose richness of color almost equals that of the Bache *Madonna*, together with the big compositions such as the Louvre *Pastoral Concert*, the Glasgow *Adulteress*, and the Prado *Madonna and Child with SS Anthony of Padua and Roch*.

The theme of the *Pastoral Concert* (plate 20)—a moment of musical diversion at sunset—is so reminiscent of Giorgione that some critics believe Titian completed a work conceived and begun by the older master. Michiel, indeed, states that paintings left unfinished at the death of Giorgione were completed by Titian (the Dresden *Venus* proves this). Yet the Louvre painting does not seem to be among them. Quite apart from similarities between the figures here (plate 21) and those in the *Miracle of the Youth's Leg* (plate 29), the dynamic compositional structure, the extension of the forms outlined in light, the sensuous luminous texture all provide an essential insight into the young Titian which is far removed from Giorgione's more intimate vision.

Even more Titianesque is the Glasgow *Adulteress before Christ* (plate 15): its subject has not even the faintest echoes of Giorgione. The excitement generated by the attitudes and gestures of the powerful, architecturally conceived figures grouped in a semicircle against the rocky background is marvelously conveyed by the wealth of chromatic planes and interplay of light and shade.

We move from the complex representation of this New Testament episode—its impact must have been even greater before the right side of the canvas was damaged (reproduction on page 50 and plate 18)—to the peaceful atmosphere of the Prado *Madonna and Child with SS Anthony of Padua and Roch* (plate 22). Here the figures are set in a limpid purity of large chromatic masses, outlined against a luminous background of wonderful tonal sequences dominated by the deep red of the Virgin's robes.

When Titian returned to Venice after his work-filled years in Padua, possibly towards the end of 1511, he found the artistic climate in the city radically changed. Giorgione had died in the autumn of 1510; Carpaccio was withdrawing more and more into isolation, his former lucid fantasy-world becoming more academic; Sebastiano del Piombo had gone to Rome, attracted by Michelangelo's titanic genius; Lorenzo Lotto had left the Veneto region to sharpen his vision in endless wanderings through central Italy. Titian, still in his early twenties, now found himself the only important rival of the aging Giovanni Bellini.

It is to this period that we can probably attribute a number of masterpieces. Looking at them now it almost seems as though in them Titian was nostalgically re-evoking the world of his master who had died so young.

So in the small altarpiece (plate 35) formerly in the Church of Santo Spirito in Isola and now at the Salute ("this panel many have believed to be by Giorgione," writes Vasari), Titian was thinking of Giorgione's small Castelfranco altarpiece with its new and free awareness of space. Titian resurrects and extends the exciting novelty of the composition—hesitantly suggested by Giorgione and then immediately countered by Sebastiano del Piombo's architectural monumentality in the *St John Chrysostom Altarpiece*—by bringing to it a freer and surer movement of forms and color masses. The saints (plates 36 and 37) are solidly placed on either side of St Mark on his high pedestal, while Mark himself is freely depicted against a cloudy sky. Sunlight, falling from the right on the statuesque figures, gives the whole composition an extraordinary feeling of spaciousness.

Almost contemporary with this altarpiece, because of similar solidity and chromatic gradations are the *Serving Woman* (plate 33), relatedly stylistically to the mother in *St Anthony Healing a Newborn Child* (plate 25)—and the so-called *Ariosto* (plate 34). Both reveal the energetic quality of Titian's temperament, even though the paintings are inspired by Giorgione. Similar, too, in form and color are the *Risen Christ* (plate 38)—formerly in the Chiesa Collection—rising like a colossus against the bright open sky, and the London *Noli Me Tangere* (plate 39). In the latter the relationship between figures and landscape which Titian has customarily kept up to this point seems to be reversed. The subtle lyricism of Giorgione's landscapes here plays no part; the unrestricted natural world, with yellow and blue tones darkening the twilight sky, do not overshadow the pathetic encounter between Christ and Mary Magdalene, her vivid red cloak billowing out around her.

This dramatic concept of humanity in which nature is subordinate was foreign to Giorgione. In the Dresden *Venus* (plate 203) we see how the symphony of curves formed by the purity of the nude figure and the silence of the spring landscape in the cold light is disturbed not only by the landscape (plate 41)—which repeats the motif of the country buildings huddled on the hill in the *Noli Me Tangere* (added by Titian, according to Michiel)—but also by the blending of white and red in the drapery and cushion that contrasts so strikingly with the delicate rosy flesh tints.

In the Pitti *Concert* (plate 45) two distinct personalities are also noticeable. Here, however, they are so obvious as to break the stylistic unity of the composition. The awkward young man on the left—the mediocre quality of execution suggests an unknown imitator rather than Giorgione himself—seems excluded from the somehow poignant interchange between the musician and the monk (plate 46). The musician is among the most memorable of Titian's figures: etched sharply, as it were, from the dark background, his head turned over his shoulder, his sensitive hands poised over the keyboard.

Titian presents an equally dramatic dialogue in the San Rocco *Christ Carrying the Cross with an Executioner* (plate 44), even though the drama here is heightened by the psychological contrast between the savage aggressiveness of the cut-throat and the perceptive gentleness of Christ. The attribution to Giorgione was corrected as early as the second edition of Vasari's *Lives of the Artists*, possibly on direct information from the artist himself. Very different is the world of feeling depicted in three other paintings: the *Gypsy Madonna* (plate 43), with its Bellini-like composition and melancholy Giorgionesque landscape—but yet so wholly Titian in the warmth and beauty of its figures; the Bath *Rest on the Flight into Egypt* (plate 42); and the Ellesmere *Three Ages of Life* (plate 48), in which the idyll of the countryside at sunset is enlivened by the innocent sleeping children, the mute conversation of the young lovers, and the old man lost in meditation.

In the Capitoline *Baptism* (plate 47) the mysticism of the event is also resolved by great insight into real life; it is idealized with a classical depth in the splendor of the tones, and the broad spatial extension of forms.

The problem of conferring on man a new classical dignity by means of color, yet at the same time conserving man's basic "earthiness," becomes Titian's increasing preoccupation in the interrupted series of masterpieces with which, by the first half of the second decade, he makes a definite break with the past. There are numerous *Sacred Conversations* exemplifying this preoccupation: in Genoa (plate 53), this being judged one of the earliest because of a certain awkwardness in the construction of the two female figures (plate 54) who recall the St Peter in the votive picture in Antwerp (plate 12); in Munich (plate 49); in Edinburgh (plate 50); and in London (plate 51). In every one of these pictures a joyous love of life is evident in the free composition of the forms. The colors are rich and splendid, while the spatial conception creates landscapes vibrant with luminous highlights and atmospheric patches of shade.

Just as warm, and idealized by means of luminous flesh tints and chromatic tones of draperies, are Titian's many female half-length paintings. These include—to note the most famous examples—the so-called Vienna *Violante* (plate 55), prototype of perfect beauty for Palma Vecchio; the Louvre *Young Woman at Her Toilet* (plate 59); the Doria *Salome* (plate 61); and the Uffizi *Flora* (plate 60).

Surging lyrically through the relationship of form and color the intensity of human life overwhelms any hesitancy previously encountered in Giorgione's works. This emotional intensity is also evident in the portraits in the New York Frick Collection (plate 56), in Copenhagen (plate 57) —which vividly recalls the Pitti *Concert* (plate 46) in the sudden turn of the head—and in the Earl of Halifax's Collection (plate 62), where the red of the sleeve lights up the dark blue of the tunic like a ruby.

An outstanding example of Titian's early chromatic classicism is generally held to be the Borghese Gallery's *Sacred and Profane Love* (plates 64–65). There have been many interpretations of this intimate, Giorgionesque picture which depicts two young women meeting at dusk by an ancient sarcophagus. Today the generally accepted theory is that the work was inspired by an episode from Francesco Colonna's *Hypnerotomachia Poliphili*. An impassioned beauty radiates from the two female figures arranged gracefully against the landscape in the horizontal rhythm of a classical frieze. The wonderfully formal harmony is achieved by the careful alternation of only a few tones: in one figure the pale rosy hues of the flesh against the vivid red of the cloak (plate 67); in the other, the red of the sleeve against the white of the dress (color plate IV). The radiant landscape provides a magnificent counterpoint. Unlike Giorgione's delicately shaded landscapes, it is painted in a dove-tailing of different colored planes: on the left, near the forbidding gloom of a wood the village buildings are illuminated by the last rays of the setting sun (plate 68); on the right, beyond the heath where mounted hunters chase game and shepherds watch their flocks, a belfry stands out against the sulphurous sunset which casts its golden reflection in the pool below.

By the middle of the second decade of the sixteenth century, when *Sacred and Profane Love* was completed and hung on the walls of Nicolò Aurelio's house, Titian had already twice refused Bembo's offer to live in Rome as painter to the Papal Court, preferring to offer his services to the Venetian Republic. His decision to consolidate his prestige on his native soil with an official appointment—a decision based also on the resultant material advantages—appeared even more sound shortly afterwards, since on Giovanni Bellini's death in 1516 Titian became the most famous and widely sought artist in Venice.

Somewhat hurriedly finished, the *Assumption* (plate 72) was placed in the choir of the Frari Church by March 20, 1518. This huge altarpiece was so revolutionary and untraditional in its concept that, according to Ridolfi, it was only the Austrian ambassador's offer to buy it that stopped the monks from rejecting the work altogether. Conceived as a central episode in an immense spatial vortex, the miraculous heavenly vision does not suggest mystical contemplation, but forces our attention on the almost exaggerated masses of figures in the foreground. The impression that the miracle is taking place in a unity of time and place is accentuated, rather than diminished by the three different foreshortenings, wonderfully united by the variations of light and the richness of the chromatic tones, graduated in a choral crescendo of polyphonic splendor. At the bottom of the picture, against a deep blue sky, blocked out in half shadow, with more violent gestures than had ever been seen in Venice, the Apostles extend their arms towards the Virgin, brightly silhouetted (plate 73) and surrounded by a circle of flying cherubs who fade into the dazzling brilliance of the sky where the silhouette of God the Father appears.

The complex freedom of composition and the plasticity of forms vibrating with inner energy reminded Dolce of the "pleasing quality and grace of Raphael," and "the greatness and *terribilità* of Michelangelo." But while it is true that even during the Fondaco and Padua frescoes, Titian was aware of the great Tuscan-Roman figurative tradition, it is equally true that in the *Assumption* he triumphantly affirms his own genius in the overpowering vitality of his color and form.

Again, he shows himself independent not only of the idealistic plasticity inherent in the geometric purity of Raphael's forms, but also of the man-centered plasticity of Michelangelo, which is based on an abstract relationship of black and white.

Work on the *Assumption* continued for a long time, and the many trials and errors gradually clarified poetic fantasy in all its lyric absolutes. We can see this in a preparatory drawing now in the Louvre, where the group of the Apostles is depicted quite differently from the same group in the painting (see page 61). During this period Titian had probably finished the *Tribute Money* (plate 76) and started the first of the *Bacchanals* for Alfonso, Duke of Ferrara (plates 78, 80 and 111). In the former the contrast between the gentle steadfastness of Christ and the sly cunning of the tempter recalls the psychological study in the earlier San Rocco *Christ Carrying the Cross with an Executioner* (plate 44); here, however, composition is made richer by the luminous intensity of the color and majestic breadth of the forms. These qualities are also outstanding in the *Sacred Conversations* in the Prado (plate 70) and in Dresden (plate 71), as well as in the Vienna *Madonna of the Cherries* (plate 77), all painted about this time.

The extraordinarily expressive vitality seen in these works is, in the two Prado *Bacchanals* (plates 78 and 80), further blended with pagan intoxication. Together with the later London *Bacchus and Ariadne* (plate 111) they decorated the study of Alfonso d'Este at Ferrara. Even though Titian kept faithfully to the literary themes he was asked to illustrate, it seems—and we have the Duke's word for this—that the artist's freedom of expression was not in the least compromised. Indeed, in the perfect synthesis of form and color, the myths seem to have taken on a renewed classicism, expressed with sensuous naturalism, but because of the relation of color between man and nature, depicted in images of ideal serenity. This rejoicing in life seems even more surprising when compared either with the motionless harmony of Bellini's *Feast of the Gods*, painted a few years earlier for the Duke's same study—a picture whose archaic preciosity even Titian (plate 110) could not modify—or, and even more to the point, with Michelangelo's tormented flights of imagination on the ceiling of the Sistine Chapel, or with Raphael's formal Platonic perfection in the earliest Vatican *Stanze*.

The *Worship of Venus* (plate 78) was inspired by a description in the fourth of Philostratus's *Images*. On the right, the ancient statue, a symbol almost of Titian's resurrection of pagan myths, rises above the exuberant tumult of young bodies, warm in the golden light. On the left, the banks of the forest surround the happy crowd of Cupids; their diagonal perspective stretching backwards and up to the most luminous of skies seems to emphasize the extraordinary variety of motifs. Yet we can still sense the cadences of perfect rhythmic movement (plate 79).

The theme of the second *Bacchanal* (plate 80)—the Dionysiac abandon of the inhabitants of the island of Andros to the effects of wine—is also drawn from a description by Philostratus. More frenzied than *The Worship of Venus*, the movements of the figures are none the less classically conceived within a solid border of color; forms dissolve and weave in and out rhythmically in depth between the lights and shadows of the forest sure of the free space in which they move. Themes borrowed from ancient sculpture and from Michelangelo are completely absorbed in marvelous bursts of warm color—an interplay of green and sulphur yellow among trees and grass, under an autumn sky whose bright turquoise patches are shot with pink and yellow. The bewitching effect of the color on the narrative makes it difficult to isolate the many fascinating details. Yet some are unforgettable: the jug of amber-colored wine held in silhouette against the sky (plate 82), or the contrast between the lilac-rose and pale blue clothing of the dancer with his back to the viewer, and his partner. There are echoes of these ideas in the work of Paolo Veronese; and the young bacchante in the foreground (plate 81), abandoned to sleep, seems, like the Ellesmere *Venus Anadyomene* (plate 90), to claim kinship with the ideal of feminine beauty to be found in the sculpture of Phidias.

Started in January 1523, the London *Bacchus and Ariadne* (plate 111) was the third and last of the mythological series painted for Alfonso d'Este. In its dynamic, sculpturally monumental composition it reveals the new direction of public taste which enabled Titian, at the beginning of the third decade, to measure his talents against Michelangelo and Raphael on their own ground. But, as in the two preceding canvases, the rich pictorial life transforms the frenzied figures into measured rhythmic cadences, and thus into an atmosphere of restrained classical eloquence. The actual as well as poetic center of the composition is Bacchus himself rushing towards Ariadne, wrapped in a purple cloak, streaming out in the wind against the azure of the sky. Ariadne (plate 112), her blue cloak bordered by her flame-red veil, is caught in an attitude of surprise as the noisy followers of the young god burst out of the wood on the other side of the picture. Leading them are a bacchante in a blue tunic and an orange cloak and a little satyr dragging with great seriousness the head of a newly sacrificed calf (plate 113). The brilliant chromatic texture, emphasized by the vibrant reds and blues, makes the unrestrained outpouring of forms modelled by golden light in their ancient ritual dance seem fixed for eternity. There is a glimpse of a magnificent landscape in the background, and the eye loses itself in the curves of sandy bays and sheer rocks beaten by the waves, in the promontories which lead away to the hills, blue in the dense mistiness of the atmosphere (plate 112).

If in the last of the *Bacchanals* for Alfonso d'Este, Titian's early chromatic classicism reaches maturity, in his religious paintings of the same period there is a new exploration of dramatic effects by means of a dynamic insertion of monumental forms in space and by more acute contrasts of light. An example of this is the altarpiece painted for the Church of San Francesco in Ancona (plate 94) and in *The Altarpiece of the Resurrection* (plates 101–105). The Treviso *Annunciation* (plate 98) is from the same period, commissioned from the artist after 1519, but quite probably an adaptation of a painting begun some years earlier—as indicated by the limpid formal serenity of the Virgin (plate 99), which is in complete contrast, both to the precise limiting of space by means of architectural perspective and to the startled impetuosity of the angel.

The pyramidal scheme of the Ancona altarpiece (plate 94), which bears the date 1520, recalls the compositional form of Raphael's *Foligno Madonna*. However, it is impossible to imagine a more radical difference than that between the architectural and imperturbable serenity of Raphael and the rampant human energy of Titian. Among dazzling golden banks of cloud, Virgin and Child are grouped with angels in a natural counterpoint of poses; the whole seems to be pitted with sudden luminous highlights. Below, the huge figures of the two saints and the donor appear dramatically outlined against the sunset: on the left is St Francis (plate 96), as passionately human as the kneeling saint in the tremendous Ansbach *Sacred Conversation* (plate 93); on the right is Alvise, leaning over the kneeling figure of Gozzi (plate 97) with a violent but propitiatory gesture. Between the two grandiose side-groups, a crooked tree, silhouetted low against the sulphurous twilight sky, bends towards the further reaches of the lagoon landscape (plate 95).

Even greater dramatic chiaroscuro gives scenic unity to the five scenes of the *Altarpiece of the Resurrection*, dated 1522 (Titian was already at work on them in 1519). In the center, the figure of Christ (plate 101), anticipating the London *Bacchus* by its statuesque projection, is a triumphant counterpoise, emerging from the darkness of night broken only by the last rays of the sunset edging the storm clouds with sinister brightness. On the right appears St Sebastian (plate 103), heavy in the shadows, compressed into the limits of the panel by his accentuated Michelangelo-like plasticity. To the left, Altobello Averoldi kneels with SS Nazarius and Celsus (plate 102), producing an almost monochrome effect by the dense, deep tones. This is a simplified structure of tremendous self-contained energy, and is to be found in just as expressive a form in the Cini Collection *St George* (plate 83). In the upper compartments, silver light illumines the Angel holding up the flaming streamer (plate 104) and the pure face of the Virgin which is hardly touched by the shadows (plate 105).

Few of Titian's portraits survive from the period between *Sacred and Profane Love* and the last of the *Bacchanals*. The magnificent Spada *Musician* (plate 84) and the Devonshire *Portrait of a Man* (plate 86) are still related to the Halifax portrait (plate 62) by the ease with which they occupy space, and by their rich chromatic texture. The so-called *Doctor Parma* (plate 85) in Vienna and the portrait presumed to be of Sannazzaro at Hampton Court (plate 87) are of a later date. They are constructed with few graduations of color between light and shade, against backgrounds of dull gray, and the psychological expression is extremely intense. The Pitti *Vincenzo Mosti* (plates 88 and 89) dates from about 1520; a pathetic and melancholy work, composed of a symphony of grays and whites modulated by the light.

After the beginning of the 1530's this Raphael-like preciosity gives way, in the male portraits in Munich (plate 106) and the Louvre (plates 107 and 108), to an unrestrained monumentality marked by great spiritual energy. We can see how Titian tends to overcome the problem of revealing his subjects by fixing their humanity in heroically idealized figures.

Although still at work on the *Altarpiece of the Resurrection* and under pressure from continuous requests from the rulers of Venice, the Duke of Ferrara, and the Marquis of Mantua—who in 1523 had become one of his great admirers—Titian applied himself for the first five years of the 1530's to the altarpiece commissioned in 1519 by Jacopo Pesaro. Erected on the Altar of the Immaculate Conception in Santa Maria Gloriosa dei Frari on December 8, 1526, with great ceremony, this canvas (plate 122) does not suffer from the fact that it was executed over a long period. To Titian's contemporaries it must have appeared just as revolutionary as the *Assumption* in so far as the traditional scheme for altarpieces was concerned.

The asymmetrical placing of the two groups of figures converging on the Virgin and the slow solemn rhythms with which the grandiose architectural elements outline and fill space find an echo in the rich and motionless clouds against the heavy mass of columns. The spatial conception of this tremendous setting is scaled down so much to human terms that the sacred scene seems actually to be taking place before the onlooker, and the transfiguration of the Divinity becomes the glorification of man.

The conscious dignity of the Bishop of Pafo and his house-hold—how self-possessed is the youngest Pesaro as he looks out from the picture—heralds the role that Titian's portraits were to play in these years: that of unsurpassed documents of contemporary life. Every portrait painted between 1525 and 1529 confirms this: the Prado *Federico Gonzaga* (plate 115) in his ample three-quarter-length pose, patting the brown-and-white dog (plate 116) that stands out so vividly against the dark-blue, gold-embroidered tunic; the Omaha *Man with Falcon* (plate 118a), an extraordinarily vital figure captured in a half-completed gesture; the Schonborn *Gentleman* (plate 118b) and the Berlin *Portrait of a Man* (plate 119b), severely aristocratic both in composition and chromatic texture; and the Dublin *Baldassar Castiglione* (plate 119a).

As the 1530's advanced, Titian's gradual absorption of Mannerist elements into his idiom was almost always success-ful. If the *St Christopher* (plate 120) in the Ducal Palace seems to compete with Giulio Romano's muscular giants, the Louvre *Laying of Christ in the Sepulchre* (plate 125) recalls the imperturbable, even though dynamically tense, serenity of its Raphael prototype, but it transforms this serenity into naturalistic eloquence by the participation of nature in the human drama. In fact, this is the sensation Titian wants to invoke, as can be seen in the fiery sunset which clothes with purple reflections the figures bent over Christ's body. A similar Pan-like feeling for nature pervades the Yarborough *Supper at Emmaus* (plate 124); the scene unfolds against the depth and spaciousness of the landscape in the dying light, and assumes the reality of everyday life. (Jacopo Bassano, for instance, took the figure of the host and the wonderful still life on the table as models.)

This new "naturalism" is notable for its more objective vision, for the changed relationship between landscape and man: instead of physically dominating the landscape, man is confidently contained within it. This results in the achievement of instances of highest art and poetry, as in the *Sacred Conversations* in London (plate 126) and in the Louvre (plate 127). In the latter, the realism with which the half-open basket containing an apple and blackberries is rendered is truly wonderful. In the Louvre *St Jerome* (plate 130), the incandescent landscape almost assumes the importance of the central figure—quite possibly as a result of the influence of northern prints which were by then familiar in Venice.

Titian was returning, with greater experience, to the subjects painted in his youth: two works now lost (Part 4, plates 188 and 190), the *Martyrdom of St Peter the Martyr*, finished in 1530 for the Church of SS Giovanni and Paolo, and the *Votive Picture of the Doge Andrea Gritti* admired by Sanudo in the Ducal Palace in 1531. Yet at the same time he was deepening the epic narrative trend he began with the Frari *Assumption* and developed in the fundamentals of the Ancona altarpiece (plate 94), the *Altarpiece of the Resurrection* and the *Pesaro Altarpiece*. The *Votive Picture of Doge Andrea Gritti* (Part 4, plate 190) repeated the motif of the *Pesaro Altarpiece* in a more condensed version of architecturally conceived human forms. We can infer this from the stupendous preparatory sketch for the St Bernardino (see reproduction on page 106).

St Peter the Martyr (Part 4, plate 188), on the other hand, showed entirely new inventiveness. The cruel death scene on the edge of a forest seems transformed into a tragedy because of the participation of the landscape "drawn in all its natural simplicity," as the admiring Vasari says. It is therefore easy to imagine how the emphasis on plastic forms in violent movement is modified by means of chiaroscuro and pictorial values and becomes the lively, natural immediacy noted by Pietro Aretino and other sixteenth-century writers. If Michelangelo saw the half-finished altarpiece during his brief Venetian stay in 1529, he must have realized how irreconcilable the dramatic spirit of Titian was with his own lonely spiritual struggle.

St Peter the Martyr was still uncompleted when Pietro Aretino arrived in Venice in 1527 and confirmed the conviction of Titian's contemporaries that the artist should be considered the equal of Raphael and Michelangelo. Similar interests and aims helped to form a lasting friendship between the famous critic and the artist. Aretino was feared rather than admired for the uninhibited quickness of his pen. (Dolce said of him: "Oh, Aretino, how lucky you are/Selling principles for money/And valuing them less than asses and oxen.") As Titian's fame grew, helped by the praises of the "secretary to the world," Aretino also benefited from his friend's rising fortunes.

The friendship between Titian and Aretino was based, however, not only on common interest, but on affinity of esthetic ideals. This is proved by many passages in the *Letters*, in which the writer describes the view towards the Rialto from his house on the Grand Canal: the continual weaving in and out of the fruit- and vegetable-laden boats; "the beautiful brides resplendent in their golden silks and jewels . . ."; the cries of the boatmen; the buildings which, in the Venetian light, seemed to be made of "unreal materials"; "the clouds made of condensed humidity" at sunset, the nearest of them alight "with the flames of the sun's fire," and those in the distance "less brilliant but still of the intensity of red-lead." In these passages the evocative force of words is obviously composed of the same raw material as Titian's paintings.

Titian's first encounter with Charles V (under the auspices

of Aretino according to Vasari, but actually arranged by Federico Gonzaga) was not successful. At the end of 1529 and the beginning of 1530, Charles was staying in Bologna to decide the fate of Italy and to be crowned King of Italy and Emperor by Clement VII. It was left to the Marquis of Mantua to comfort Titian after the artist's hopes had been shattered, and he added 150 ducats from his own pocket to the only commission Charles gave Titian: a portrait of himself. Two years later, however, during his second stay in Bologna during the winter of 1532–33, the Emperor was convinced of Titian's art and openly expressed his admiration by naming him official portrait painter, Count of the Lateran Palace, Palatine Count of the Aulic Council and the Consistory, Knight of the Order of the Golden Spur—this last being a title which gave the painter the much coveted privilege of free access to the Court, and conferred on his sons the rank of Nobles of the Empire.

The many privileges conceded and especially the friendliness of the powerful monarch consolidated Titian's fame abroad as well as in Italy, and helped to foster the artist's dealings with his illustrious patrons, among whom the Dukes of Urbino had been since 1532 outstanding in their generosity.

During these years Titian's activity in the field of portrait painting assumes a particular importance. In the previous decade, it had progressed to an heroic objectivity in its subjects, very different from the majestic, idealized objectivity of Raphael, and poles apart from the loving, probing, psychological approach of Lotto and Moroni's poetic faithfulness to the truth. The capacity of embodying in ever more refined and magnificent paintings the "ideal" character of the sitter corresponded exactly to society's desire for dignity and splendor. Such was the evocative force of color in depicting his sitters as ideal types that Titian could sometimes do without the actual physical presence of the sitter, basing his portrait on that of other artists, medallions, or even on a simple description of the sitter's physical features (as in the portrait, now lost, of Cornelia, lady-in-waiting to Countess Pepoli).

Caught for eternity is *Charles V with His Dog* (Prado; plate 132). The portrait was executed in 1533, and the full-length figure, with its attitude of regal authority, is a symphony of golden browns and light grays in the full dress. Outstanding, too, are the portraits of *Cardinal Ippolito de' Medici* in the Pitti Gallery (plate 133), and the so-called *Titian's Father* in the Ambrosiana (plate 134): the first in "Hungarian" costume, a parade portrait in wonderfully deep tones of violet. The second, simple in its frontal pose, is resolved by the clear red of the military uniform.

Executed between 1534 and 1538 were the Vienna *Isabella d'Este* (plate 139), a retrospective figure, splendidly dressed; the Louvre *Francis I* (plate 145), a figure reflecting tremendous aggressive vitality; *Francesco Maria della Rovere* (plate 142) and *Eleonora Gonzaga* (plate 143), both in the Uffizi. They are shown in all their princely regalia—the one seated in her magnificent gala costume of white and black and gold, yet with melancholy reflected on a face past its youthful prime; the other posed heroically in his armor, which glints in the light against a dark red curtain—as much a synthesis of warrior virtues as is the *Alfonso d'Avalos* in the De Ganay Collection (plate 144).

A contrast to the nobility of these portraits is provided by the freshness of *La Bella* (color plate III, Part 2); a composition still in classic vein, a perfect harmony of aristocratic feminine beauty and rich play of blues, blacks, golds and purples. The same unknown model reappears in the *Venus of Urbino* (plate 155) and again in the Vienna *Girl in a Fur* (plate 140), the simplicity of her pose molded by warm light, the unstressed color relationship between the pinks of flesh and the reddish-blonde of fur—which in the later version in Leningrad (plate 141) is enriched by the strawberry red of a feathered hat.

In the Uffizi *Venus of Urbino* (plate 155), executed in 1538 for Guidolbaldo della Rovere, the immediate comparison which we make with the Dresden *Sleeping Venus* (plate 203) in fact heightens the basic and radical difference which exists between them. No longer sleeping innocently against a gentle magical landscape, the woman is now stretched out in lazy abandonment, animating the room with her provocative feminity. The little dog curled up asleep, the servants busy selecting clothes (plate 156), the decorative plant on the sill in front of the window through which can be seen patches of sky—these are wonderfully realistic comments on the surroundings and lend reality to the sensuous scene.

Similar sensuality expressed in lyrical terms is to be found in the open landscape of the Louvre *Pardo Venus* (plate 153), which definitely belongs to the late 1540's. We need only note Titian's attitude to nature (plate 154), which here resembles the treatment I have already commented upon in several religious pictures of the same period.

In two important works, the Vatican *Virgin and Saints* (plate 136) and the Verona *Assumption* (plate 137), the rich drama of the huge altarpieces of the Frari (plate 72) and Ancona (plate 94) seems to be smothered by soft modulations of color and by the elaborate affectation of its formal treatment. For even Titian sometimes seems affected by Mannerist inflections—the Uffizi *Madonna* (plate 129) and the Louvre *Allegory* (plate 131) are instances. We come, then, to the *Presentation of the Virgin in the Temple* (plates

148–49), executed between 1534 and 1538 for the Sala dell'Albergo in the Scuola della Carità. In the broad stage-like unfolding of the composition, the public spectacles by Vittore Carpaccio seem to be renewed—but how very much more solemn and dignified is Titian's pictorial story-telling. The picture is composed of magnificent pictorial sections connected to each other with sure, professional, almost academic ability; sections which dazzle the onlooker by the richness and variety of their tones; the wonderful portrait groups executed with objective immediacy (plate 150); the awesome scenery of Titian's native valleys (plate 152); the old woman (plate 151) crouched against the staircase which the Virgin, shown here as a young girl, climbs self-possessedly, surrounded by a golden aura.

The artist used elements of form belonging to the Mannerist repertory and this is also revealed in the over-emphatic classicism of parts of the *Presentation* (Venice Accademia) and perhaps more obviously, and not always resolved into pictorial values, in several works now lost but recorded for the years 1537 and 1538. Thus, while light and shade dramatized the vitality and exuberance of the *Annunciation* (Part 4, plate 189)—sent as a gift to the Empress Isabella in 1537—the rhetorical formalism of the *Caesars* (Part 4, plate 191) commissioned by Federico Gonzaga in 1537, was in a Mannerist style that was acceptable to artistic circles in Mantua dominated by Giulio Romano. Very differently, in the famous "battle" in the Ducal Palace (Part 4, plate 192), started in 1513, left, not resumed until 1537, and finished the following year, the various hints of Mannerism, as the drawings in the Louvre and the Uffizi testify (see pages 109–110) were transformed by means of chiaroscuro into a lively play of movement. We are reminded by this of the print of the *Crossing of the Red Sea* (page 110), published in 1549, but drawn by Titian probably in the second half of the 1530's.

Following the San Rocco *Annunciation* (plate 157), basically a quiet and serene work in naturalistic surroundings, Titian seemed towards the middle of the century to embrace Mannerism openly—almost as though he wanted to discover its essence.

The result was the Prado *Address of Alfonso d'Avalos* (plate 158), finished in 1541, and the Vienna *"Ecce Homo"* (plate 174), dated 1543, both strongly oratorical works in which we also find a fine awareness of historical reality. Also in this group are: the Louvre *Christ Crowned with Thorns* (plate 170), an interweaving of sculptural forms bound together by a use of light that was to be an example for Tintoretto; *St John the Baptist* (plate 172) in Venice, a masterpiece of academic *bravura*, enlivened by the freshness of the luminous landscape (plate 173); the processional standard of Urbino (plates 176 and 177), in which the miracle of the central panel at Brescia (plate 101) is no longer repeated; the ceiling of the School of San Giovanni Evangelista, now in Washington (plate 178), and the three canvases of the Salute (plates 179, 180 and 181).

So much overpowering plasticity and labored theatricality as well as the violent exaggerations of colors definitely reflect the taste of contemporary Venetian artistic circles. They were continually drawn by the problems of form and composition of the Mannerists of Central Italy, introduced in nearby Mantua by Giulio Romano, and in Venice itself by Sansovino, Vasari, and the Salviati. But Titian did not accept Mannerism in all its distortions and formulas, but rather modified it for his own needs. He used it to emphasize his humanistic vision.

The Venice *St John the Almsgiver* (plate 187), which can be dated 1545, already indicates by its mastery of plastic tension the point where—with respect to previous works—we can see more color against the background shadows, which are treated with a delicate sfumato. It is a preciosity which no longer binds the tones together with rich brilliance, but, more simply, in the dense luminosity of the atmosphere (plates 188 and 189). Following his Mannerist experiences Titian resumed his style of transposing natural realism into an idealized idiom by means of this synthesis of light and color which condenses all values of form and space. However, we sense a spiritual uneasiness which up to now had not troubled his serene vision of man's destiny.

Now in his mature phase, Titian reiterated the absolute autonomy of the expressive value of color and closed the dialogue he had since his very first paintings with the Tuscan-Roman tradition. With the passage of time he had disagreed with it more radically, and in the 1550's the crisis became consciously felt. He would now go on steadfastly without looking back, offering living proof to Paolo Pino, Biondo, and Dolce in their controversy with Varchi, Doni, and Vasari, on the superiority of color over drawing, of painting over sculpture, of Venice over Rome.

To the years in which the crisis was being resolved belong some memorable examples of Titian's portraits, characterized by a raw sincerity: there is no trace of compromise for the sake of adulation. After *Cristoforo Madruzzo* of São Paulo (plate 163), depicted full length, as is also the so-called *Mendoza* in the Pitti (plate 162), which is, however, more intensely individualized, there are the Berlin *Clarissa Strozzi* (plate 166) and the Washington *Ranuccio Farnese* (plate 167). The first is a most refreshing portrait of early youth, and the second elegant in his refined costume but with a melancholy expression on his face, as if he were already aware of the weight of his destiny. The Naples *Paul III* (plate 168) was probably executed by Titian at Busseto in 1543. The old man is turned in a three-quarter pose towards the onlooker, indomitable will expressed in every line of his face (plate 169). It is a haunting study and this quality is emphasized by the expressive values of the wine-red of the cloak against the dead white of the surplice, all rendered with broad brush-strokes.

Although the frontal pose is static, and painted with restrained chromatic density, the so-called *Young Englishman* in the Pitti (plate 192) emerges from the half-shadows with intense vitality, conveyed through the enigmatic green eyes which immediately fix the onlooker's attention. The incomparable way in which Titian "catches character unaware" is shown in other portraits: the Ottawa *Daniele Barbaro* (plate 190) and the Pitti *Pietro Aretino* (plate 193). If Barbaro's moral and intellectual virtues seem to be personified in the singular nobility with which he is portrayed, the violent, cynical character of Titian's friend is depicted with almost cruel honesty by the broad execution and the huge body filling the canvas, over which the head towers, turned to the right as though in sudden angry reproach.

Aretino is easily recognized in this "awesome marvel." He himself praised the portrait in a letter to Duke Cosimo in October 1545: "Certainly it breathes, pulsates, and moves the spirit in the same way that I do in life." He complains, however, that "if I had paid him more, truly the cloth would have been shining, smooth and stiff, like satin, velvet and brocade." One realizes from this malicious comment that not even Titian's close and enthusiastic friend had fully grasped how the artist was silently and purely reaffirming the dominance of color over the intellectual formalism of the Tuscan-Roman Mannerist school. But the comment may have been written in a fit of pique at Titian's absence from Venice, for after a short stay in the Marches with the Duke of Urbino, in the autumn of 1545, Titian abandoned his comfortable home in Venice to go to Rome.

BIOGRAPHICAL NOTES

1488–90. Birth of Titian. The Vecellio family came from Pieve di Cadore. Tommaso, the founder, a notary at Pozzale, moved in the second half of the thirteenth century to Pieve di Cadore, where from 1290 onwards he appears in the records with the title of "Dominus" or "Messere," an indication of his being either affluent or well known. One of his sons, Guecello or Vecello, also a notary, appears as mayor of Cadore from 1321 to 1326. From a grandson of his, Guecello or Vecellio, a notary, is derived the surname of his descendants, many of whom were active in local public life. Count Vecellio, Titian's grandfather, was a jurist and one of the heads of the government of the Cadore "Magnificent Community." On February 23, 1508, when he was already past middle-age, he refused to surrender to the forces of Emperor Maximilian, who were later defeated at Valle di Cadore on March 2 of the same year. Gregorio, one of his sons, was Captain of the Century of Pieve from 1494 to 1507. His wife Lucia gave him two sons and three daughters: Francesco, *Tiziano*, Orsola, Caterina and Dorotea. The exact dates of birth of Francesco and Titian are not known. The first report comes from Dolce, who records the fact in 1557 that Titian executed the frescoes of the Fondaco dei Tedeschi (1508) "when he was not yet twenty years old." Titian therefore would have been born in 1488. Vasari's comment (1568) at the end of his list of Titian's works "up to the age of about 76," also presupposes this date— actually 1490. The writer must certainly have obtained direct information during his Venetian stay in 1566. Other contemporary evidence puts the artist's birth between 1473 and 1482. Titian himself, writing on August 1, 1571, to Philip II about some money owed him, tries to enlist the royal sympathy by invoking his "age of 95." But the artist's claim does not coincide with any of the dates supplied to Philip II by his secretary Garcia Hernandez: 1474, in letters of October 11, 1559, and October 15, 1564; 1479, in that of November 20, 1561 (Beroqui, 1946). The note in the Register of Deaths in the Parish of San Canciano, found recently by Lotti, makes it 1473. In this way, while Titian was still alive, a tradition of his exceptional longevity began, and this tradition was accepted without question by all art historians up to the beginning of this century. After the first doubts were expressed by Cook in 1902, it was Hourticq in 1919 who showed, after a detailed critical re-examination, how improbable was the date of 1477 given as exact by Anonimo del Tizianello (1622), by Ridolfi (1648), and backed by Cavalcaselle in 1877. Other reasons aside—including the fact that Titian wished to add a few years to his age in order to increase his prestige—the theory that the artist was born between 1488 and 1490 is the most acceptable one (and the one usually agreed on today), because of the basic fact, quite rightly emphasized by Dell'Acqua, that only by assuming this late date "does the early activity of Titian become plausible. It avoids the difficulty, particularly great in dealing with a painter possessing such overwhelming gifts, of presupposing a long period of inactivity, or of trying to fill this period with the few pictures that for stylistic reasons are dated before 1510." In this case, the birth of Titian's brother Francesco, the elder by two years, must also be put later. According to Dolce's evidence, Titian, then nine years old, moved with Francesco to Venice where, after going from the workshop of Sebastiano Zuccato to that of Gentile and Giovanni Bellini, he chose Giorgione, the "newest" painter then in Venice, as his master. (For a recapitulation of this whole question, cf. V. Basch, *Titien*, second ed., Paris; and, more recently, Pallucchini.)

1508. Frescoes on the south and east façades of the Fondaco dei Tedeschi. The old Fondaco burned down on January 28, 1505. In May 1507, the work of reconstruction was already at roof-level, and was completed in May of the following year. On December 11, 1508, Lazzaro Bastiani, Vittore Carpaccio and Vettore di Matteo valued the frescoes of the Fondaco dei Tedeschi at 150 ducats. Twenty ducats were subtracted from this amount, with Giorgione's approval. Although Titian's name does not appear on the documents along with Gior-gione's, there is no doubt but that he was his collaborator, according to both Dolce's and Vasari's reports.

1510. Death of Giorgione, in the autumn.

1511. Frescoes in the Scuola del Santo in Padua. On December 1, 1510, Titian's name appears in the account books of the Scuola del Santo in Padua, but the artist did not begin to paint the three miracles of the saint until April 25, 1911. On December 2 of the same year he received four gold ducats from the Scuola "for the remaining and final payment for the three pictures."

1513. Invited to Rome as painter to the Papal Court by Pietro Bembo, Titian declines the offer, and prefers to offer his services to the Venetian Republic. He agrees to decorate the Sala del Gran Consiglio without pay, beginning with the *Battle*, which, because of its awkward placing between two windows on the wall towards the piazza, was an undertaking that "no man, until now, has wanted to attempt." He asked, however, for the first appointment to the Brokerage of the Fondaco dei Tedeschi to become vacant, with the same benefits of the Salt Office which were enjoyed by Giovanni Bellini: the payment for two assistants and the necessary materials for painting. His conditions were accepted, and the artist opened a workshop at San Samuele, where his assistants were Antonio Buxei and Ludovico di Giovanni; the latter was formerly an assistant of Giovanni Bellini. Thus Titian begins his relationship with the Venetian Republic—a relationship frequently fraught with controversy because of his reluctance to fulfill his obligations punctually.

1514. At the instigation of other Venetian painters—Giovanni Bellini, now an old man, probably among them—on March 20 the Council of Ten takes from Titian the concessions granted to him in 1513. In November they give back these concessions, at his renewed request. The license of the Fondaco dei Tedeschi, though, was given him only in 1517, after the death of Giovanni Bellini.

1516. Death of Giovanni Bellini. Brother Germano, Prior of the Convent of the Frari, commissions Titian to paint *The Assumption* altarpiece for the big altar in the main apse of the Church of Santa Maria Gloriose dei Frari. The relationship begins between Titian and the Court of Ferrara, where he is documented as being, with his assistants, from January 31 to March 22.

1517. The concession of the Brokerage Office of the Fondaco dei Tedeschi, previously Giovanni Bellini's, exempts Titian from annual taxes, and gives him a salary of twenty-five ducats, and another twenty-five ducats for every portrait of a new Doge to be hung in the Sala del Maggior Consiglio. Titian was given various small services to perform by Alfonso I d'Este, Duke of Ferrara: the design for a balcony, the acquisition of antiques; he was also working on a picture representing "a bath."

1518. On March 20, the Feast of St Bernardino, the altarpiece of The Assumption was solemnly unveiled in the Church of the Frari. From correspondence between Giacomo Tebaldi, the Ferrarese ambassador to Venice, and Alfonso I d'Este, we gather that Titian was working on a painting to be hung in the study of the castle at Ferrara. The exact subject had been chosen by the Duke; the painting was probably the first of the three *Bacchanals*: the *Worship of Venus*.

1519. On April 24, Jacopo Pesaro, Bishop of Pafo, signed the contract with Titian for the altarpiece of the Assumption in Santa Maria Gloriosa dei Frari commissioned the previous year. The *Pesaro Altarpiece* was finished in 1526. Titian was late in delivering the painting for Alfonso I d'Este's study. The Duke wrote to his agent Tebaldi on September 29 in an impatient and threatening manner; Titian hurried to Ferrara with the painting, and was at the d'Este Court on October 17.

1520. Date of the altarpiece commissioned by Alvise Gozzi for the Church of San Francesco in Ancona (*Madonna and Child, Two Saints, and the Donor*). On behalf of the Duke of Ferrara, Titian interested himself in majolica vases and glassware. He was at Ferrara, repairing the damage done to one of his pictures by an inept varnishing. He painted the St Sebastian as part of the polyptych commissioned by the Papal Legate, Altobello Averoldi, neglecting the paintings promised to Alfonso I d'Este (probably the *Bacchanal* and the *Bacchus and Ariadne*). The Duke reacted somewhat violently, and, at the insistence of his Venetian ambassador, Titian agreed to send to Ferrara the *St Sebastian* painted for Averoldi. The Duke, however, afraid of incurring the enmity of the powerful Papal Legate, refused to accept the painting.

1521. Titian goes to Brescia, and was probably active in Conegliano and Vicenza.

1522. The polyptych commissioned by Averoldi is finished. Although warned that he must continue his work in the Sala del Maggior Consiglio in the Ducal Palace, or lose all his concessions, Titian does not, however, take up this work again until the following year. Instead, he paints the portrait of Antonio Grimani, elected Doge in 1521. Tebaldi announces to Alfonso I d'Este that Titian is working on the *Bacchus and Ariadne*.

1523. In February, he is at Ferrara a few days after the arrival of one of his paintings (probably the *Bacchus and Ariadne*) at the d'Este Court. The beginning of his relationship with the Court of Mantua; his first painting for the Marquis Federico Gonzago was a portrait. Death of Antonio Grimani and election of Andrea Gritti, whose portrait Titian painted. According to tradition, the newly elected Doge has Titian fresco the *St Christopher* on the stairway of his private apartments.

1524. After much hesitation, Titian goes to Ferrara, where he stays from November through the beginning of 1525. Giulio Romano establishes himself at the Court of Mantua. Titian came to know him during his frequent stays with the Gonzaga family.

1525. He marries Cecilia, with whom he has been living for some time, and by whom he has had two sons

Pomponio and Orazio. The Doge Andrea Gritti appoints Titian's father, Gregorio Vecellio, Superintendent of the Mines; the artist's brother-in-law, Matteo Soldano, is nominated Chancellor at Feltre.

1526. The *Pesaro Altarpiece*, commissioned in 1519, is finished for the Church of Santa Maria Gloriosa dei Frari.

1527. Pietro Aretino arrives in Venice, where he is joined by Sansovino and Sebastiano del Piombo, as a result of the Sack of Rome. Titian, through the intervention of Pietro Aretino, offers to Federico the portraits of Aretino himself and of Girolamo Adorni, Charles V's ambassador at Venice, who had died in 1523. The Marquis consents on October 11 to Aretino's entreaties to reward Titian.

1528. Stay at Ferrara. He wins the competition (in which Palma Vecchio and Pordenone were also competing) organized by the Confraternity of San Pietro Martire for his altarpiece depicting St Peter the Martyr, which was to replace the former one by Jacobello del Fiore on the altar in the Venetian Church of SS Giovanni and Paolo.

1529. Coronation of Charles V on February 25. Either at the end of 1529 or (and more probably) at the beginning of 1530, Titian executes his first portrait of Charles V at Bologna. He was paid one ducat for it, to which Federico Gonzaga added 150 from his own pocket. On April 27, the altarpiece together with *St Peter the Martyr*, commissioned two years earlier for the Church of SS Giovanni and Paolo, was commenced. On August 5 his wife Cecilia dies. In September he sends Federico Gonzaga, now Duke of Mantua, a copy of the *St Sebastian* from the Brescia polyptych, and also the portrait of Cornelia, lady-in-waiting to Countess Pepoli.

1531. Jacopo Sansovino executes silverwork from Titian's designs for the Court of Mantua. Titian receives from the Duke the living at Medole for his son Pomponio, who was pursuing an ecclesiastical career. In September he transferred his workshop from San Samuele to the house at Birri Grande in the district of San Canciano.

1532. The beginning of Titian's relationship with Francesco Maria I della Rovere, Duke of Urbino and Captain General in the pay of the Venetian Republic. Sebastiano Serlio was the intermediary between Titian and Gian Giacomo Leonardi, the ambassador of Urbino to Venice, who mentions that Titian was working on a figure of Christ, a *Nativity*, and a portrait of Hannibal—all for the Duke of Urbino. Charles V is in Italy again at the end of the year.

1533. During the early months of the year Charles V is at Bologna, where Titian paints a second portrait of him. This second meeting had important consequences for the artist. On May 10, the Emperor gave Titian a diploma, naming him "Count of the Lateran Palace, of the Royal Council and of the Consistory," with the title of Palatine Count. He was also named Knight of the Golden Spur, with sword, chain, and golden spur, and the right to enter the Court. His sons receive the title of

"Nobles of the Empire," and are given privileges equal to those who had had titles for four generations.

1534. Death of Alfonso I d'Este, Duke of Ferrara. He is succeeded by his son Ercole II. In the *Nativity* Titian had been at work on since 1532 arrives at Pesaro for the Court of the Duke of Urbino. He paints Isabella d'Este as a young girl, taking a previous portrait by Francia as his model.

1535. In March, the other works commissioned in 1532 arrive in Pesaro. These are the figure of Christ and the portrait of Hannibal which Leonardi had seen half-finished in Titian's studio in 1532.

1536. In Venice, Titian begins the portrait of the Duke of Urbino, whose armor he had received, and probably also that of the Duchess Eleonora who was in Venice from September until the first months of the following year. Federico Gonzaga decides to decorate one of the rooms of his castle in Mantua with portraits of the *Twelve Caesars*, for which Titian had already received the commission.

1537. Ercole II, Duke of Ferrara, withdraws a portrait of his father Alfonso from Venice. Titian offers as a present to Empress Isabella, wife of Charles V, an *Annunciation* which had been refused by the nuns of Santa Maria degli Angeli at Murano. Four of the *Twelve Caesars* arrive in Mantua. Titian was asked for the others in the years immediately following.

1538. Death of Francesco Maria della Rovere. Titian enters into a closer relationship with his successor

45

Guidobaldo II, who had given him commissions when he was Duke of Camerino. Because he is overdue in delivering the "canvas" of the *Battle*, a painting to be placed near it is commissioned from Pordenone, and the Brokerage appointment of the Fondaco dei Tedeschi is taken away from Titian.

1539. Pordenone dies in January, and on June 23 the Brokerage appointment of the Fondaco dei Tedeschi is given back to Titian. He executes the portrait of the Doge Pietro Lando, Andrea Gritti's successor on his death in 1538. Leonardi notifies Guidobaldo II that Titian has almost finished three portraits: of Charles V, Francis I of France, and the "Great Turk Suliman."

1540. Titian paints the portraits of Alessandro degli Organi (from whom he receives an organ in exchange); Pietro Bembo, for the second time; and Vincenzo Cappello, commander-in-chief of the Venetian fleet. Death of Federico Gonzaga, Duke of Mantua.

1541. He finishes the *Address of D'Avalos*, Marquis del Vasto, who had commissioned the picture from him during the winter of

1539. He paints the portrait of Don Diego Mendoza, Charles V's ambassador to Venice. In August he obtains from Charles V in Milan a pension of 100 ducats. Giorgio Vasari stays in Venice in December 1541 and during the first months of 1542.

1542. He executes the portraits of the twelve-year-old daughter of Roberto Strozzi, and of Ranuccio Farnese. He finishes a *Nativity* for the Cathedral of Novara, and paints a votive picture in honor of the Doge Lando.

1543. He is present in Ferrara at the meeting of Charles V and Paul III, whose portrait he painted.

1544. He delivers a portrait of Isabella of Portugal, deceased wife of Charles V, to Mendoza.

1545. In Venice he paints portraits of Daniele Barbaro, of Guidobaldo II of Urbino, and of Pietro Aretino —who sends his own portrait to the Grand Duke Cosimo in Florence. In September Titian is in Pesaro and Urbino as guest of Guidobaldo II, and begins the Duchess Guilia di Varana's portrait—which, however, remains unfinished because of her death.

TITIAN'S PAINTINGS

Plate 1

LUCRETIA. *Canvas, 122.5 × 58.* *
Formerly in Munich, Fleischmann Gallery. Longhi (1946) and Pallucchini accept the attribution to Titian put forward by Suida. This is the painting nearest in style to the Fondaco dei Tedeschi frescoes (1508). See plates 186 and 187 in Part 4, Lost Paintings.

Plate 2

PORTRAIT OF A MAN. *Canvas, 75 × 62.5. Washington, National Gallery of Art, Kress Collection.* Formerly in the Henry Doetsch Collection in London, and the Goldmann Collection in New York. After an X-ray examination Burroughs (1938) has pointed out the existence of three versions which he attributes to Giorgione. Richter (1942) attributes only the first to Giorgione and the restoration to Titian. Morassi (1942) remarks on affinities with Cariani and inclines, with reservations, towards the Giorgione attribution. However, the portrait—already attributed to Giorgione by Cook in 1906 —is today generally considered to be by Titian according to Berenson's exact indications (1894). It is very close to the Fondaco dei Tedeschi frescoes and there are many obvious analogies with the oldest Titian portraits, including the *Serving Woman* and the so-called *Ariosto* in the London National Gallery (plates 33 and 34). See also plate 3.

Plate 3

PORTRAIT OF A MAN. Detail: the face.

Plate 4a

THE BIRTH OF ADONIS. *Panel, 35 × 162. Padua, Museo Civico.* Originally the front of a *cassone*. Acquired through the Emo Capodilista bequest of 1864 (Grossato, 1957). This and the panel below were traditionally ascribed to Giorgione by the Capodilista family. Attributed to Giorgione by A. Venturi (1893) and Cook (1900), the paintings were attributed to Cariani by Schmidt (1908) and to Romanino by L. Venturi (1913), followed by A. Venturi in 1928 and Berenson in 1932. Although the names of Romanino (Zampetti, 1955, second edition) and Lorenzo Lotto are put forward even today, the attribution of the two paintings to the young Titian, as proposed by Morassi (1942, 1954), is the most likely one. Pallucchini, who earlier (1946) doubtfully attributed the two paintings to Cariani, is now in favor of Titian before 1511, as is Longhi. See also plate 5.

Plate 4b

THE FOREST OF POLYDORUS. *Panel, 35 × 162. Padua, Museo Civico.* Originally the front of a *cassone*. Cf. note to plate 4a, and see also plates 6 and 7.

* All dimensions are given in centimeters

Plate 5
THE BIRTH OF ADONIS. Detail: the four figures round the tree.

Plate 6
THE FOREST OF POLYDORUS. Detail: the two figures on the left.

Plate 7
THE FOREST OF POLYDORUS. Detail: the decapitated man between two figures.

Plate 8
ORPHEUS AND EURYDICE. *Panel, 39 × 53. Bergamo, Accademia Carrara, Lochis Collection.* Long thought to be by Giorgione or an imitator, this picture is now recognized as being an authentic Titian dating from before 1510 by Longhi (1927 and 1946), Suida, Morassi (1942 and 1954) and Pallucchini. It appeared with the attribution to Titian at the "Giorgione and his School" Exhibition in Venice (P. Zampetti, 1955), and has recently been attributed to Palma Vecchio by Coletti (1955). See also plate 9.

Plate 9
ORPHEUS AND EURYDICE, *Bergamo*. Detail: the two figures in the background at the right.

Plate 10
ST PETER, POPE ALEXANDER VI AND BISHOP PESARO. *Canvas, 145 × 183. Antwerp, Musée Royal des Beaux-Arts.* At the bottom an inscription of doubtful authenticity: "RITRATTO DI UNO DI CASA PESARO IN VENETIA CHE FU FATTO GENERALE DI SANTA CHIESA. TITIANO F. C." This picture represents Pope Alexander VI, who holds a flag with the Borgia arms on it, recommending to St Peter Jacopo Pesaro, Bishop of Pafo and Commissioner of the Papal Galleys which, together with the Venetian fleet (this can be seen about to set sail in the background), routed the Turks at Santa Maura on June 28, 1502. The painting (seen by Van Dyck in a Venetian church, as is borne out by a leaf in his sketchbook (G. Adriani, 1941)) is recorded in the Collection of Charles I of England, then in the Monastery at St Pascal in Madrid. William I of Holland gave it to the museum in Antwerp in 1823. Because the picture has an ex-voto character in connection with the victorious Battle of Santa Maura in 1502, and also because of the fact that the next year the hated Borgia pope died, Cavalcaselle dates it 1501–3, L. and A. Venturi 1502, and Gronau 1503. It is traditionally dated at the beginning of the century. Hourticq (who believes the picture was started by Giovanni Bellini and finished by Titian) dated it 1515. Suida thinks it was executed at two different times: the whole outline and the St Peter enthroned about 1512, and the patron, the donor Jacopo Pesaro, and the landscape about 1520 —this also on the basis of a comparison with the Ancona altarpiece. Pallucchini, while accepting the hypothesis of its execution at two different times, dates the canvas earlier, 1508–9, with Longhi (1946), and limits the second intervention after 1520 to the bas-relief (plate 11) and the lagoon in the background. See also plates 11 and 12.

Plate 11
ST PETER, POPE ALEXANDER VI AND BISHOP PESARO. Detail: the bas-relief and helmet. Ozzola (1932–33) remarks that the design of the helmet is certainly later than 1505, and therefore dates the picture about 1510 on the grounds of this external evidence.

Plate 12

ST PETER, POPE ALEXANDER VI AND BISHOP PESARO. Detail: St Peter's head.

Plate 13

MADONNA AND CHILD. *Panel, 46 × 56. New York, Metropolitan Museum, J. S. Bache Collection.* Formerly in the Collections of the Earls of Exeter, and of Benson, and of Lord Duveen of Millbank. Ascribed to Titian in the period before he did the Paduan frescoes (1511) by Berenson (1928), Suida, Longhi (1946) and Pallucchini, this picture has many points of similarity with the New Haven *Circumcision* (plate 14).

Plate 14

THE CIRCUMCISION. *Panel, 36.7 × 79.3. New Haven, Yale University Art Gallery.* The attribution to Titian before 1511 accepted by Berenson, Longhi (1946) and Morassi (1954) is accepted also by Pallucchini—with reservations, however, because of the panel's bad state of preservation.

Plate 15

THE ADULTERESS BEFORE CHRIST *Canvas, 137 × 180. Glasgow, Corporation Galleries.* Possibly identifiable as the *Adulteress* mentioned as being by Giorgione in Camillo Sordi's letter written from Venice to Francesco Gonzaga in 1612 (Luzio, 1913). Paintings on a similar subject are recorded, always with the name of Giorgione, in the inventories of Michele Spietra's Collection in Venice in 1656, Giovanni Vincenzo Imperiale's Collection in Genoa in 1661, the Pesaro brothers' Collection in Venice in 1663, and in a private collection in Florence in 1672. The first reliable information about this Glasgow painting is dated 1689, when it is listed as a Giorgione in Queen Christine of Sweden's Collection. In 1721 it was attributed to Pordenone, and in 1856 was acquired by the Glasgow Gallery. After Cavalcaselle (1871) cast doubt on the attribution to Giorgione, proposing Cariani instead, the canvas was given various attributions: to Sebastiano del Piombo by Bernardini (1908), Lionello Venturi (1913), Coletti (1955) and Della Pergola (1955); to Romanino by A. Venturi (1928); to Domenico Mancini, with reservations, by Zampetti (1955). However, the very real problem of the attribution of this painting, varying between the traditional attribution to Giorgione (Bode; Morelli, 1880; Cook, 1900; Justi, 1908; Richter, 1937) or the one to Titian (Berenson, 1928 and 1932; R. Longhi, 1927; Suida; Fiocco, 1941; Morassi, 1942; Pallucchini, 1944) must be resolved in Titian's favor in view of a decisive comparison with the Paduan frescoes, and especially with that of the *Miracle of the Newborn Child.* The restoration carried out by Ruhemann (1955), which has persuaded Hendy (1954) and, unaccountably, Berenson (1954) to return to the Giorgione attribution, has revealed that Christ's halo is in the shape of a cross. Thus the recent proposal of E. Tietze-Conrat (1945) that this painting represents *Susannah Declared Innocent by the Prophet Daniel,* which this scholar holds to be one of the four stories of Daniel commissioned by Alvise da Sesti from Giorgione in 1508 according to a contract made known by Molmenti but of dubious authenticity according to Richter—this proposal must be dismissed. On the basis of a copy of the composition in the Accademia Carrara in Bergamo, reproduced here (canvas, 140 × 219), Berenson (1928), has

Fischel, and Gronau (Richter, 1937) to Giorgione. It was exhibited with the Giorgione attribution in Baltimore (de Batz, 1942) and in Venice (Zampetti, 1955). The portrait so similar in tonality to the Bache *Madonna* (plate 13) and the Glasgow *Adulteress* (plate 15), is attributed to Titian by Suida, Morassi (1942), Pignatti (1955), and Longhi (Zampetti, 1955).

ascertained that the original was mutilated, that there was the figure of a young soldier on the right-hand side, and at the same time has identified a fragment of this figure in the Sachs Collection in New York, here given as plate 18. See also plates 16 and 17.

Plate 16
THE ADULTERESS BEFORE CHRIST Detail: the man in the right foreground.

Plate 17
THE ADULTERESS BEFORE CHRIST Detail: the woman.

Plate 18
BUST OF A YOUNG SOLDIER. *Canvas, 54.5 × 43.5. On loan to the National Gallery, London, from the Sachs Collection, New York.* Fragment of the figure of a young man originally at the right of the canvas of *The Adulteress before Christ* in Glasgow (cf. note to plate 15).

Plate 19
PORTRAIT OF A WOMAN. *Canvas, 31.7 × 24.1. New York, Duveen Collection.* In the nineteenth century, this painting was in the Lichnowsky Collection in Kuchelna, Czechoslovakia; then in that of Lord Melchett in Romsey, Hampshire. Baldass (1929) attributes it to Cariani; Richter (1932), Mayer (1932),

Plate 20
PASTORAL CONCERT. *Canvas, 110 × 138. Paris, Louvre.* Originally this may have been in Isabella d'Este's Collection; the work was sold to Charles I of England by the Duke of Mantua in 1627. Acquired in 1649 by the French banker Eberhard Jabach, it became part of the Collection of Louis XIV in 1671. After Waagen (1839) had suggested Palma Vecchio, thus casting doubt on the traditional attribution to Giorgione to which Morelli remained faithful (1880), Crowe and Cavalcaselle (1871) assigned the canvas to an imitator of Sebastiano del Piombo, and L. Venturi (1913) to Sebastiano del Piombo himself in a Giorgione mood. Rejecting the untenable attributions to Palma Vecchio and Sebastiano del Piombo, critics today are divided between Giorgione and Titian. Supporting the first are A. Venturi (1928), B. Berenson, Justi (1936), Gronau, Richter (1937), Fiocco (1948), Tietze, L. Venturi (1954) having revised his 1913 opinion, Hendy (1954), and Coletti (1955). The attribution to Titian made by Lafenestre (1909) is taken up—with more valid proof, however—by Hourticq, Suida, Morassi (1942), Longhi (1946), Pallucchini (in spite of the fact that he recognizes a Giorgione-like outline), and Zampetti (1955). Hourticq

suggests the theory that the painting was started immediately after the Padua frescoes of 1511 and finished after 1530, and that it is thus identifiable in the picture of *Nudes* for the Duke of Mantua: see Lost Paintings, 1530, *Nude Female Figures*. As with the Glasgow *Adulteress* (plate 15), it is again the Padua frescoes which offer the most decisive basis for the attribution to Titian of this much-discussed picture. See also plate 21.

Plate 21

PASTORAL CONCERT. Detail: the heads of the two young men in the center.

Plate 22

MADONNA AND CHILD WITH SS ANTHONY OF PADUA AND ROCH. *Canvas, 92 × 103. Madrid, Prado.* Towards the middle of the seventeenth century this picture was offered to Philip IV of Spain by the Duke of Medina, Viceroy of Naples. In 1657 it is mentioned as being in the Sacristy of the Escorial, and by the hand of "Bordonon." Velasquez judged it to be by Pordenone; Cavalcaselle attributes it first to this artist and then to Francesco Vecellio. Rightly attributed to Titian by most critics, from Wickhoff to Dell'Acqua, it is believed to be Giorgione's work by Justi (1936), Berenson, Richter (1937), Oettinger (1944), Gamba (1954) and Coletti (1955)—all of them following Morelli's suggestion.

Plate 23

ST ANTHONY HEALING A NEW-BORN CHILD. *Fresco, 320 × 315. Padua, Scuola del Santo.* The subject is the newborn child's evidence miraculously obtained by St Anthony in favor of the mother who has been unjustly accused by her husband. With the two frescoes which follow

(plates 26 and 30), this is the first documented work of Titian which survives (Gonzati, 1852, first edition). Already on December 1, 1510, the artist's name appears in the account book of the Scuola (E. Rigoni, 1941), but he did not start work until April 23 of the following year (E. Grazzini Cocco, 1927). The last receipt of payment for "the three pictures," signed "TICIAN DI CADOR," is dated December 2, 1511. The frescoes have recently been the object of intense study by A. Morassi (1956). See also plates 24 and 25. As noted on page 15, the *Triumph of Faith*, known through the woodcut here shown on pages 56 and 57, is to be dated to Titian's stay in Padua.

Plate 24

ST ANTHONY HEALING A NEW-BORN CHILD. Detail: the group of figures on the left.

Plate 25

ST ANTHONY HEALING A NEW-BORN CHILD. Detail: the mother's head.

Plate 26

THE MIRACLE OF THE YOUTH'S FOOT. *Fresco, 327 × 220. Padua, Scuola del Santo.* The subject is the miraculous healing of the young man who had punished himself for kicking his mother by cutting off his foot. See also plates 27, 28 and 29.

Plate 27

THE MIRACLE OF THE YOUTH'S FOOT. Detail: the first four heads on the left, together with that of the kneeling woman.

Plate 28

THE MIRACLE OF THE YOUTH'S FOOT. Detail: the landscape on the upper left side.

Plate 29
THE MIRACLE OF THE YOUTH'S
LEG. Detail: the head of the young
man on the left of the saint.

Plate 30
THE JEALOUS HUSBAND. *Fresco,
327 × 183. Padua, Scuola del Santo.*
A preparatory sketch for the foreground scene of this fresco, but with
changes in its composition, is
preserved at the École des Beaux-
Arts in Paris (pen drawing, 18.8
× 17.7, reproduced here). See also
plate 31.

Plate 31
THE JEALOUS HUSBAND. Detail:
the foreground scene.

Plate 32
PORTRAIT OF A MAN. *Canvas,
50.2 × 45.1. New York, Metropolitan
Museum.* Formerly the property of
the Grimani family in Venice, then
in the W. Savage Collection in

London, and in the Altman Collection in New York, where it was
attributed to Giorgione in 1913 by
Bode. R. Longhi's attribution to
Titian is accepted by Suida, Phillips
(1937), Morassi (1942), Pallucchini,
and Pignatti (1955). Richter (1937)
believes it probably by Palma
Vecchio.

Color Plate I
PORTRAIT OF A MAN. Detail of
plate 34.

Plate 33
PORTRAIT OF A WOMAN (THE
SERVING WOMAN). *Canvas, 117 ×
97. London, National Gallery.* It bears
the artist's initials: "T. V." Recorded
in 1641 in the house of Martinengo
Colleoni in Brescia, then in the
Crespi Collection in Milan, and
the Cook Collection in Richmond.
The identification of the portrait with
Caterina Cornaro proposed by H.
Cook (1915) is not based on valid
arguments. Cook believes the painting was started by Giorgione and
finished by Titian. Formerly attributed to Giorgione and to B.
Licinio, the work is today generally
considered an early Titian (C.
Holmes, 1914–15; C. Gould, 1959).
Tietze compares the canvas with the
Portrait of a Man (plate 2) and with
the so-called *Ariosto* (plate 34), and
notes a similarity to the mother in
the *Miracle of the Newborn Child* fresco
in the Scuola del Santo in Padua
(plate 23). In the bas-relief, the
woman is drawn in profile.

Plate 34
PORTRAIT OF A MAN (ARIOSTO).
*Canvas, 81.2 × 66.3. London, National
Gallery.* On the parapet: "T. . . . . .
V." Formerly in the Collection of
Alfonso Lopez, possibly also in Van
Dyck's Collection, this picture was

acquired from Lord Darnley's Collection at Cobham Hall in 1904. It was famous as far back as the seventeenth century, and known by Rembrandt and Sandrart (Tietze; C. Gould, 1959). The old identification with Ariosto is highly doubtful (Gronau, 1933); the identification with the gentleman of the Barbarigo family noted by Vasari, as proposed by J. P. Richter (1895), is not certain either—however fascinating it may be. Although Wickhoff (1904) has put forward the name of Sebastiano del Piombo, and Cook and Richter (1937) Giorgione's, most critics today consider the portrait to be the work of the young Titian, between 1508 (Tietze) and 1511–12 (Pallucchini).

Plate 35

ST MARK ENTHRONED WITH FOUR SAINTS (*Cosmas and Damian, Roch and Sebastian*). *Panel, 230 × 149. Venice, Church of Santa Maria della Salute, Sacristy.* Recorded by Vasari as being in the Church of Santo Spirito in Isola, for which it was painted as an ex-voto—probably at the end of the 1510 plague (Fogolari, 1935). From 1656 on it has been at the Salute. Dated by Gronau after the 1504 plague, and by Fogolari after the one of 1510, the painting today is generally considered to date from the period immediately following Titian's work in Padua (Pallucchini), as Cavalcaselle previously suggested. Recently, Morassi (1954) has dated it before 1511. See also plates 36 and 37.

Plate 36

ST MARK ENTHRONED WITH FOUR SAINTS. Detail: the busts of SS Cosmas and Damian.

Plate 37

ST MARK ENTHRONED WITH FOUR SAINTS. Detail: the busts of SS Roch and Sebastian.

Plate 38

THE RISEN CHRIST. *Canvas, 133 × 82.* Formerly in the Gallery of Archduke Leopold William (1660), then in the Raikewich Collection (?) and the Crespi Collection (1914 sale catalog), and finally in the Achillito Chiesa Collection in Milan, it was sold at an auction in New York in 1926. Frizzoni (1906) attributes it to Palma Vecchio; R. Longhi (1927) was the first to recognize it as being a masterpiece by the young Titian. Pallucchini compares it with the Altarpiece of St Mark in the Salute (plate 35) and with the "*Noli me tangere*" in London (plate 39). Connected with this picture is the drawing shown here (charcoal and chalk, 41.9 × 26.5) now kept in the Uffizi.

Plate 39

"NOLI ME TANGERE." *Canvas, 107 × 90. London, National Gallery.* Mentioned by Ridolfi in 1648 as being by Titian while in the Muselli Collection in Verona, it passed to the Orléans Gallery in 1727. In 1855 it came to the National Gallery in London with the Rogers bequest (C. Gould, 1959). Cavalcaselle, Hetzer, and most contemporary critics ascribe the painting to the young Titian—according to Morassi, before 1511. Richter (1937) and Tietze believe they see in it a painting conceived by Giorgione and finished by Titian between 1511 and 1515. During its recent restoration, X-ray examination has revealed a different pose for the figure of Christ (C. Gould, 1958). See also plate 40.

Plate 40

"NOLI ME TANGERE," *London.* Detail: the landscape on the upper right side.

Color Plate II

"NOLI ME TANGERE". Detail of plate 39.

Plate 41

SLEEPING VENUS *by Giorgione. Canvas (transferred in 1843 from the original canvas), 108.5 × 175. Dresden, Detail of the landscape.* Today there is almost unanimous agreement that Titian added the landscape, together with the figure of Cupid (uncovered and then covered up again during the restoration of 1843, and attested to by X-ray examination: G. Gamba, 1928–29; H. Posse, 1931), to the *Venus* seen by Michiel in 1525 in the house of Gerolamo Marcello (see Part 2, plate 203, Attributed Paintings).

Plate 42

REST ON THE FLIGHT INTO EGYPT. *Panel, 46.5 × 64. London, Collection of the Marquess of Bath.* Formerly attributed to Schiavone, it is rightly believed by Suida and Pallucchini to be one of the first of Titian's many *Sacred Conversations* with open landscape backgrounds. A second version is in the Contini Bonacossi Collection in Florence (see Part 2, plate 200, Attributed Paintings).

Plate 43

THE GYPSY MADONNA. *Pane, 65.8 × 83.8. Vienna, Kunsthistorisches Museum.* Formerly in the possession of Archduke Leopold William. While criticism today agrees on the attribution to the young Titian—only A. Venturi and Cook suggest Giorgione, though Richter (1934) believes in Giorgione's intervention in the initial stages of the painting —the date of this work is controversial. Cavalcaselle places it at the end of the fifteenth century, Fischel at 1502–03, Tietze at about 1510, and Wilde (1930) and Rothschild (1932) at around 1520. Pallucchini points out that while the compositional structure is obviously inspired by Bellini (Detroit *Madonna* of 1509, and Brera *Madonna* of 1510), as previously mentioned by Suida, the pictorial material is much nearer to works which can be dated to several years later than 1510. This is the most plausible date for the picture, even though it must be kept fairly close to the Padua frescoes and the Prado *Madonna and Saints* (plate 22). A. Venturi believes it to have been executed shortly after the addition of the landscape to Giorgione's Dresden painting (plate 41), since the same landscape, with a few changes, is found in this Venetian *Madonna*. There is an old copy of it with Titian's signature in the gallery of the Accademia dei Concordi in Rovigo.

Plate 44

CHRIST CARRYING THE CROSS WITH AN EXECUTIONER. *Canvas, 70 × 100. Venice, School of San Rocco.* Recorded already in 1519 as being in the Church of San Rocco, this canvas is the one mentioned by Michiel in 1532 when he noted in the house of Antonio Pasqualigo a painting by Giorgione or one of his students derived from the San Rocco canvas—thereby seeming to say that this San Rocco canvas was Giorgione's work. Vasari in 1550 attributes it to Giorgione, but in his second edition, of 1568, after mentioning the canvas in the life of Giorgione, he says explicitly in the life of Titian: "For the Church of San Rocco he painted ... a picture of Christ with the Cross on his shoulder with round his neck a rope pulled by a Jew, the figure of whom many people have thought to be by the hand of Giorgione, and who is the object of the greatest interest in Venice today." Noted as being Titian's work by Ridolfi, Boschini and Sansovino (G. Lorenzetti, 1920), Cavalcaselle in 1877, Wickhoff in 1895, and Gronau in 1908 all took the name of Giorgione under consideration again, and critical opinion was in agreement—except for Hourticq and Suida, who dissented. Since the Venetian exhibition of 1935 devoted to Titian (Fogolari), the attribution to this artist, with a date of the second decade of the sixteenth century, has gained ground (Morassi, 1942; Fiocco, 1948; but in collaboration with Giorgione; Tietze, Pallucchini, Gamba, 1954; Pignatti, 1955). L. Venturi (1954), Zampetti (1955) and Berenson (1957) have still attributed this picture to Giorgione.

Plate 45

CONCERT. *Canvas, 108 × 122. Florence, Pitti Palace.* Possibly identifiable in a painting admired by Ridolfi in the Collection of Paolo del Sera. In 1654 it was acquired as Giorgione's work by Cardinal Leopoldo de' Medici, and from his collection eventually passed to the Pitti Palace. Today it is mostly thought to be Titian's work, and was exhibited as such at the Venetian exhibitions of 1935 (Fogolari) and 1955 (Zampetti), after Morelli (1886) had ascribed it to Titian's youth (about 1515)—thus casting doubt on the traditional attribution to Giorgione. Pallucchini seems to agree, with reservations, to Gronau's hypothesis that this is a picture started by Giorgione (the young man with the feathered hat) and finished by Titian. Fiocco (1848) and L. Venturi (1954) have gone back to the Giorgione attribution, still upheld by Cavalcaselle and Justi. Tietze-Conrat (in *Gazette des Beaux-Arts*, S. VI, vol. 27) proposes instead the name of Sebastiano del Piombo, also mentioned by Hourticq and Friedeberg. A still less likely attribution, to Domenico Campagnola, is put forward by Morelli, Wickhoff (1895) and Hadeln. See also plate 46.

Plate 46

CONCERT. Detail: the head of the musician in the center.

Plate 47

THE BAPTISM OF CHRIST. *Canvas, 115 × 89. Rome, Capitoline Museum.* Recorded as being Titian's work by Michiel in 1531, in the house of the Spanish merchant Giovanni Ram who is portrayed at the right of the painting in the act of praying. Cavalcaselle ascribes the canvas to Paris Bordone; Dussler (1935) and

Triumph of Faith woodcut (see page 15 and the comments on plate 23).

Hetzer (1920) also cast doubts on its attribution to Titian. Pallucchini dates it about 1512, Tietze about 1516: its stylistic resemblance to the *Three Ages* (plate 48) make the first dating more probable.

Plate 48

THE THREE AGES OF LIFE. *Canvas, 106 × 182. Edinburgh, National Gallery of Scotland, loan of the Earl of Ellesmere* (1955). Formerly in Augsburg, then in the Collection of Queen Christine of Sweden in the second half of the seventeenth century, it was sold in 1722 by Prince Odescalchi to the Duke of Orléans, in whose collection it remained until 1798. Hetzer (1920) considers it a copy, but it is certainly the original version (A. L. Mayer, 1937), of which many copies are known—there is one in the Galleria Doria in Rome. It is usually dated about 1515 (Tietze), being generally considered the painting mentioned by Vasari as executed by Titian on his return to Ferrara for the father-in-law of Giovanni da Castel Bolognese. Longhi (1946) on the other hand, noting how the three sleeping cherubs on the right served Romanino for his plaque of the *Innocents* in the frame of the great altarpiece dated 1513 and now in the Museo Civico in Padua, dates the picture, with good reason, slightly earlier than 1513.

Plate 49

MADONNA AND CHILD, ST JOHN THE BAPTIST, AND THE DONOR. *Canvas, 75 × 92. Munich, Bayerische Staatsgemäldesammlungen.* In the Gallery of the Archduke Leopold William in 1659, it then passed to the Collection of the Elector John William of Düsseldorf, possibly as a gift from Emperor Joseph I. Morelli and Gronau consider it to be a copy by Titian's school; according to Voll it is a copy by another artist of an original known only through the engraving (Alte Pinakothek catalog, 1936). Cavalcaselle's attribution to Titian is rightly accepted by Berenson and Pallucchini, among others. A late copy, with variations, is preserved in the Bucharest Museum. As an example of Titian's interpretation of landscape, an engraving of the *Sacrifice of Isaac* by Ugo da Carpi from a sketch of Titian's is here reproduced.

Plate 50

MADONNA AND CHILD, ST JOHN THE BAPTIST, AND THE DONOR. *Canvas, 90 × 120. Edinburgh, National Gallery of Scotland, loan of the Earl of Ellesmere.* Formerly in London, at Bridgewater House. Morelli first recognized this painting as being by the young Titian. However, Cavalcaselle does not agree with this attribution—he is undecided among Palma Vecchio, Bernardino Licinio and Polidoro Lanzani; nor does Tietze or Hetzer (1920: he thinks it was executed by a painter under Titian's influence around 1530–40, while he holds that the version in the Glasgow Gallery—which Suida takes as coming from the workshop of Titian—is nearer to the master). Morelli (1886), Ricketts and Mayer date the picture about 1510–12, Suida a few years later, while Pallucchini puts it after the *Sacred Conversation* in Casa Balbi in Genoa (plate 53).

Plate 51

THE HOLY FAMILY AND A SHEPHERD. *Canvas, 99 × 137. London, National Gallery.* Admired by Van Dyck, who made a pencil sketch of it (G. Adriani, 1941), this painting was, at the beginning of the nineteenth century, still in the Borghese Palace in Rome, where it had been recorded in 1693 (C. Gould'

1959). From 1831 it has been on view at the National Gallery in London. Inexplicably attributed to Paris Bordone by Oettinger (in *Magyar Müveszet*, 1931) and by Tietze as a result of a comparison with the picture on the same subject in the Louvre, this painting was, according to Heinemann (1928), started by Titian in his youth, given further touches in 1517–19, and finished by an unknown artist. As for the preceding picture, dating for this one varies between 1510 and 1512 (Gronau) and about 1516 (Mayer).

Plate 52

TARQUIN AND LUCRETIA. *Pane, 84 × 68. Vienna, Kunsthistorisches Museum.* Possibly identifiable in the painting noted by Ridolfi, it is recorded as belonging to Charles I of England, and then to Archduke Leopold William. The traditional attribution to Titian (E. Egarth in 1858 proposed Palma Vecchio instead; see E. R. Engerth, 1882) was taken up again by Suida (1927) and Longhi (1927), although many critics disagreed with this attribution in spite of close affinities with the half-figure compositions in Munich, Paris and Rome (plates 58, 59 and 61). The copy (no. 963) in the Pitti Palace could be by Padovanino.

Plate 53

MADONNA AND CHILD, TWO SAINTS, AND A WORSHIPPER. *Canvas, 130 × 185. Genoa, Collection of Marchese Balbi di Piovera.* Properly judged as one of the most successful masterpieces of Titian's youth by Morassi in 1946, up to that date this painting was noted only by Cavalcaselle and Gronau. Pallucchini rightly dates it slightly later than the *Baptism of Christ* in the Capitoline Museum in Rome (plate 47). The two saints are Catherine and Dominic See also plate 54.

Plate 54

MADONNA AND CHILD, TWO SAINTS, AND A WORSHIPPER. Detail: St Catherine.

Plate 55

PORTRAIT OF A YOUNG GIRL (VIOLANTE). *Panel, 64.5 × 51. Vienna, Kunsthistorisches Museum.* There is no foundation for the identification of this girl with Palma's daughter Violante. The picture has been mutilated on the right and at the bottom, as can be seen from the engraving in the *Theatrum Pictorium* of Teniers (1660), where it is attributed to Palma Vecchio. This attribution remained until Longhi (1927), followed by Suida, rightly ascribed the panel to Titian. This attribution may be confirmed by a comparison with the St Catherine (plate 54) of the Balbi *Sacred Conversation* (Pallucchini).

Plate 56

MAN IN A RED CAP. *Canvas, 79 × 68. New York, H. C. Frick Collection.* Formerly in the Lane Collection, Dublin. While Tietze omits it in cataloging Titian's works, and Coletti has recently put forward the name of Giorgione (1955), the attribution to Titian proposed by Berenson (1932) is generally accepted today. Placed by Morassi (1954) before the Padua frescoes, the painting is dated by Pallucchini after 1515 because of its likeness to the small portrait in the Städel Institute in Frankfurt which bears on the back the date 1516 (see plate 202, Part 2, Attributed Paintings).

Color Plate III

CONCERT. Detail of plate 45.

Plate 57

PORTRAIT OF A MAN. *Canvas, 80.5 × 66.5. Copenhagen, Statens Museum for Kunst.* Belonging in 1828 to a Swedish collection, this painting was acquired by the Copenhagen museum in 1912. The most likely date for its execution is that of 1513–14 as proposed by Suida and Tietze and accepted by Pallucchini, who points out its affinity with the monk at the harpsichord in the Pitti *Concert* (plate 46).

Plate 58

VANITY. *Canvas, 98 × 81. Munich, Bayerische Staatsgemäldesammlungen.* From the Collection of Emperor Rudolph II in Prague, it passed to the Collection of the Elector in Munich. Formerly attributed to Saviati (1748 at Schleissheim), to Palma Vecchio and to Giorgione (up to 1884 in the Alte Pinakothek), and to Giorgione or Pordenone by Cavalcaselle, this painting was re-attributed to Titian by Morelli (1880). Pallucchini has recently agreed, if doubtfully, to the suggestion put forward by Hetzer (1920) and Tietze that it may be an old copy. Tietze dates it about 1512–16. Mayer believes the painting to have been transformed in the seventeenth century from "Sibyl with a Book" into "Vanity with a Mirror" on the basis of the so-called *Sibyl of Marostica* published by Cook (1926).

Plate 59

YOUNG WOMAN AT HER TOILET. *Canvas, 96 × 76. Paris, Louvre.* From the Gallery of the Gonzaga family in Mantua to the Collection of Charles I of England, and from there to Louis XIV's. The many identifications suggested—"Titian's Mistress" (in the Collection of Charles I), "Alfonso d'Este and Laura Dianti" (Ticozzi), "Federico Gonzaga and his Mistress Isabella Boschetti" (Hourticq, 1919)—are unconvincing, especially since the most plausible date for this picture's execution is 1512–15, i.e. earlier than Titian's relationship with the courts of Ferrara and Mantua (Tietze).

Plate 60

FLORA. *Canvas, 79 × 63. Florence, Uffizi.* Sold by Don Alfonso Lopez, Spanish ambassador at Amsterdam, to the Archduke Leopold William. In 1793 it passed from Vienna to the Uffizi during an exchange of pictures. Sandrart, who made an engraving of the picture when it was still in the possession of Don Alfonso Lopez, is responsible for the title of this magnificent female figure.

Plate 61

SALOME. *Canvas, 90 × 72. Rome, Doria Gallery.* Formerly in the Collections of Prince Salviati, Queen Christine of Sweden, and Prince Odescalchi, it went to the Doria Gallery in 1794. Cavalcaselle (1878) attributes it to Pordenone and Justi (1908) to Giorgione, but today critical opinion is almost unanimous in calling it an authentic work of the young Titian, as suggested by Morelli (1897). Among the many versions of this painting, that formerly in the Benson Collection in London is considered by Burckhardt (1898) to be of better quality than the Doria canvas. However, Tietze rightly considers the former Benson version a late copy executed by Titian's workshop, with variations on the Doria original.

Plate 62

PORTRAIT OF A YOUNG MAN. *Canvas, 100 × 84. London, Collection of the Earl of Halifax.* Formerly in the Collection of Edward Wood at Temple Newsan. The indisputable attribution to Titian around 1515 first put forward by Gronau is accepted by most critics. However, Hetzer (1920) does dispute this, as do Richter (1937) and Fischel, while H. Debrunner (1928) for some strange reason suggests Lorenzo Lotto. The painting was exhibited at the "Italian Art and Britain" exhibition in London in 1960, still with an attribution to Giorgione or Titian.

Plate 63

PORTRAIT OF LUDOVICO ARIOSTO *Canvas, 59.5 × 45.5. Indianapolis, J. Herron Art Institute.* This picture appeared for the first time at a sale at Sotheby's in London on January 29, 1929; it later went to the Booth Tarkington Collection in Indianapolis. Identified as a portrait of Ariosto (Catalogue of the Exhibition at Toledo, Ohio, 1940) by comparison with the painting formerly in Casa Oriani at Ferrara, and with the engraving in the 1532 edition of *Orlando Furioso*, in which Ariosto looks older (Wilbur B. Peat, in *The Bulletin of the Art Institute of Indianapolis*, 1947). Tietze, who accepts the suggestion that this is the portrait mentioned by Ridolfi as being in the possession of the painter Nicolò Renieri, dates it about 1516, as does Pallucchini—this latter critic, however, not offering an opinion as to who painted it. Berenson (1957) recognizes it definitely as an authentic Titian.

Plates 64–65

SACRED AND PROFANE LOVE. *Canvas, 118 × 279. Rome, Borghese Gallery.* Probably part of Scipione Borghese's purchase, through his treasurer, Cardinal Pallavicini, of seventy-one pictures in 1608 from Cardinal Sfondrato. This painting has been listed under various titles in the inventories and catalogues of the Gallery: "Adorned and Unadorned Beauty" (Francucci, 1613); "Three Loves" (Manilli, 1650); "Profane Love and Sacred Love" (1693); "Divine and Profane Womanhood" (Rossini, 1700); and finally "Sacred and Profane Love" (Vasi, 1792, and Fidecomisso, 1833). Its subject also has been variously interpreted: as an illustration from part of Valerio Flacco's *Argonautica* and representing Venus persuading Medea, according to Wickhoff (1895); as Violante, the presumed daughter of Palma and Titian's mistress, in her double role of Violante and of Venus, according to Gerstfeld (1910); as Polia and Venus from the *Sogno di Polifilo*, according to Hourticq (1917) and Panofsky (1930). Clerici (1918) suggests that the subject comes from Francesco Colonna's *Sogno di Polifilo*, and Friedländer (1938), Wischnitzer-Berstin (1943) and Della Pergola (1955) agree. Mayer (1939), who agrees with Friedländer's hypothesis, thinks that the subject was suggested to Titian by Bembo, and identifies the coat of arms as that of Nicolò Aurelio, whose family had already been mentioned in this connection by Gnoli (1902). Venturi's hypothesis, therefore—that the picture, painted for Alfonso d'Este, came from Ferrara—will not hold. The canvas is usually dated about 1515; De Logu (1947) and Argan (1950) have made it the subject of intense study. See also plates 66–69 and color plate IV.

Plate 66

SACRED AND PROFANE LOVE, *Rome.* Detail: child and sarcophagus.

Plate 67

SACRED AND PROFANE LOVE, *Rome.* Detail: nude female figure.

Plate 68

SACRED AND PROFANE LOVE, *Rome.* Detail: landscape to the left.

Plate 69

SACRED AND PROFANE LOVE, *Rome.* Detail: landscape to the right.

Plate 70

MADONNA AND CHILD, AND SS ULFUS AND BRIDGET. *Panel, 86 × 130. Madrid, Prado.* The authenticity of this painting, already established in the sixteenth century as being by Titian, is doubted by Von Hadeln (1908: D. Campagnola), Hetzer (1920) and Tietze. Cavalcaselle and Gronau believe it to be Titian's work before 1508, Longhi (1927) dates it about 1510, while Pallucchini considers it to be contemporary with the Frari *Assumption* (plate 72).

Plate 71

SACRED CONVERSATION. *Panel, 138 × 191. Dresden, Gemäldegalerie.* It represents the Madonna and Child, with St John the Baptist (left), SS Paul, Mary Magdalen and Jerome (right), and probably came from the Grimani ai Servi house in Venice into the collection of the d'Este family in Modena. Cavalcaselle makes a strange attribution to Andrea Schiavone; Hetzer (1920) rejects the Titian attribution and ascribes the panel to his school about 1510. Morelli was the first to re-attribute it to Titian, and most critics today agree with this, dating it to 1515–18.

Plate 72

THE ASSUMPTION OF THE VIRGIN. *Panel, 690 × 360. Venice, Santa Maria Gloriosa dei Frari.* Signed: "TICIANVS MDXVI." It was commissioned from Titian in 1516 by the Prior of the Frari Convent, and solemnly in-augurated on March 20, 1518, as Sanudo records. From 1818 to 1919 it was on loan at the Accademia. Two drawings relating to the panel are known: the first, in the Louvre and reproduced here, is a sketch for the group of the Apostles (pen drawing, 23.1 × 30.2); the other, in the British Museum in London, is a study for the figure of St Peter (black pencil, 15.7 × 13.5). See also plates 73–75.

Color Plate IV

SACRED AND PROFANE LOVE. Detail of plates 64–65.

Plate 73

THE ASSUMPTION OF THE VIRGIN. Detail: the Madonna.

Plate 74

THE ASSUMPTION OF THE VIRGIN. Detail: the angels, upper left.

Plate 75

THE ASSUMPTION OF THE VIRGIN. Detail: the Virgin's head.

Plate 76

THE TRIBUTE MONEY. *Panel, 75 × 56. Dresden, Gemäldegalerie.* Signed: "TICIANVS F." Mutilated at the sides, as a copy in the Accademia di San Luca in Rome proves, it is almost certainly identifiable as the painting executed, according to Vasari, for the door of one of Alfonso d'Este's studies. The Ducal Collections in Modena acquired the painting in 1746, and it is described there in 1657 by F. Scanelli. The date of 1516 proposed by Hetzer (1920) is generally accepted (after Ricketts had earlier advanced the traditional dating of 1508–14 first proposed by Cavalcaselle). A copy attributed to Garofalo is in the Uffizi.

Plate 77

THE MADONNA OF THE CHERRIES. *Panel (transferred from canvas), 81 × 99. Vienna, Kunsthistorisches Museum.* It comes from the Collection of the Archduke Leopold William, where it is recorded as being in 1659. According to Tietze-Conrat (*Der reife Dürer*, No. 326), the obvious connection this picture has with the *Madonna of the Siskin* (painted by Albrecht Dürer in 1506 while he was staying in Venice) can be explained by an identical source of inspiration represented by an already extant Venetian prototype. The datings proposed by Cavalcaselle (before 1508), Hetzer (about 1506), Gronau

61

(1512–15) and others are rightly pushed forward by Pallucchini to about 1516–18. During the transfer, it became evident that the final version hides an earlier composition with noticeable differences. There is a record of this earlier version in a copy by Erasmo Engert (Tietze, fig. 33).

Plate 78
THE WORSHIP OF VENUS (THE CHERUBS). *Canvas, 172 × 173. Madrid, Prado.* Part of the decoration of Alfonso d'Este's study, this picture was taken by the Legate Cardinal Aldobrandini in 1598 to Rome, together with the *Bacchanal* also in the Prado, and the *Bacchus and Ariadne* in London (cf. notes to plates 80 and 111). In 1639 it was offered, together with the *Bacchanal*, to Philip IV of Spain through the Viceroy Monterey. According to the express wishes of Duke Alfonso d'Este, the subject faithfully follows the description of one of the paintings dedicated to the Eroti in the sixth book of Philostratus' *Immagini*, as recorded by Ridolfi. Most probably it can be identified with the first of three paintings commissioned by Alfonso for his study—and more exactly with the picture started in 1518 and finished in October 1519, as can be inferred from the voluminous correspondence between the artist, the d'Este Court, and its representatives in Venice. In proposing the dating of 1516–18 for this canvas, Tietze puts forward the hypothesis that the copy with variations in the Stockholm museum does not derive from the painting now in the Prado, but from a second version of it. See also plate 79.

Plate 79
THE WORSHIP OF VENUS (THE CHERUBS). Detail: the little cherubs in the lower left corner.

Plate 80
BACCHANAL (THE ANDRIANS). *Canvas, 175 × 193. Madrid, Prado.* Signed: "TICIANUS F." The sheet of music carries the words: "Qui boit et ne reboit, ne sais que boire soit." This picture (like the previous one) was painted for Alfonso d'Este's study, was in Rome in 1598, and was offered to Philip IV in 1639. Titian also partly based this canvas on a passage from Philostratus' *Immagini*, where he describes the picture with Dionysus arriving by sea at the island of Andros where the inhabitants are awaiting him in a state of intoxication (Wickhoff, 1902). Datable to between 1518 and 1519 (*Worship of Venus*, plate 78). Tietze, who has pointed out an exact derivation from Michelangelo (the bacchante stretched out next to the young woman raising a cup, taken straight from a cartoon for the *Battle of Càscina* in the Leicester Collection), proposes a dating of about 1518, and, basing his theory on a Rubens copy, believes there may be a second version (cf. note to plate 111). See also plates 81 and 82.

Plate 81
BACCHANAL (THE ANDRIANS). Detail: the naked bacchante, bottom right.

Plate 82
BACCHANAL (THE ANDRIANS). Detail: the central group.

Plate 83
ST GEORGE. *Panel, 124 × 65. Venice, Cini Collection.* Formerly in the Collection of Sir Andley Neeld, then at Agnew's in London. Waagen (1854) believed it to be by Giorgione; Spahn (1932) does not agree with the attribution to Palma Vecchio ad-

vanced by Borenius, Fiocco, and Gronau; L. Venturi (1954) and M. Calvesi (1956) return to the Giorgione attribution; R. Longhi (1936 and 1956), followed by Tietze, Morassi, and Pallucchini, attributes it to Titian. Longhi proposes a dating of about 1511, while Tietze believes the painting to be a fragment of the picture commissioned from Titian in 1517–22 for the Viscount de Lautrec (see Lost Paintings). With this late dating, accepted by most critics, the panel was exhibited in Venice in 1955 at the "Giorgione and his School" exhibition (Zampetti).

Plate 84

PORTRAIT OF A MUSICIAN. *Canvas, 99 × 81.8. Rome, Spada Gallery.* Attributed to Giorgione by Hermanin in 1933, after his decision in 1931 that it was by Titian, this painting is identified by Porcella (1931), without any stylistic reason as *Battista Ceciano, the Bass Viol Player*, recorded by Vasari as having been executed by Orazio, Titian's son, in Rome in 1546. In the Spada Gallery Catalog of 1954, Zeri reconfirms the attribution of the painting to Titian, dating it (with good reason) about 1515–20. Zampetti, in the Catalog of the Giorgione Exhibition (1955), proposes a dating of 1510–15.

Plate 85

PORTRAIT OF A MAN. *Canvas, 88 × 75. Vienna, Kunsthistorisches Museum.* Recorded as being by Titian in the *Theatrum Pictorium* (1660) of the Collection of the Archduke Leopold William. Today, little credit is given to the identification of the sitter with the doctor Parma, whose portrait is noted by Ridolfi. The canvas was deleted from the catalog of Titian's works by Cavalcaselle, Hetzer and Tietze, attributed to

Domenico Campagnola by Wickhoff (1893), and to Giorgione by Cook and Justi. Given back to Titian about 1511 by Morelli, and to this artist about 1528 by Ozzola (1939), this portrait is rightly considered by Pallucchini to be close to the supposed portrait of Sannazzaro at Hampton Court (plate 87), and thus datable to the early 1630's.

Plate 86

PORTRAIT OF A MAN. *Canvas, 81 × 68.5. London, Collection of the Duke of Devonshire.* At one time attributed to Giorgione, this canvas is doubtfully attributed by Cavalcaselle to either Lotto or Cariani; Cook and Berenson hold it to be by the latter artist. Longhi made it known in 1927 as a Titian dating to about 1515, while Pallucchini proposes a dating of 1515–20.

Plate 87

PORTRAIT OF A MAN OF LETTERS. *Canvas, 84 × 72. Hampton Court, Royal Collection.* At one time held to be a portrait of Alessandro de' Medici, the work is believed by Gronau to portray the poet Jacopo Sannazzaro, on the basis of a copy bearing this name. Suida, with good reason, opposes this identification, observing that there is no resemblance at all to the known portraits of Sannazzaro, born in 1458. The attribution to Titian is accepted by most critics, although rejected by Hetzer (1920) and Tietze. The canvas, generally dated between 1511 and 1520, is believed by Mayer to date from 1515 to 1520; Pallucchini shortens the period to 1518–20.

Plate 88

PORTRAIT OF VINCENZO MOSTI. *Canvas (transferred from panel), 85 × 66. Florence, Pitti Palace.* On the reverse of the painting, not in

Titian's hand: "Tommaso Mosti di anni xxv l'anno MDXXVI Titiano de Cadore Pittore." The identification of the sitter as Tommaso Mosti has been demonstrated as historically untenable by A. Lazzari (1952), who thinks it more probably represents Vincenzo Mosti, a gentleman active at the Court of Duke Alfonso d'Este, named a count in 1526, and dying in 1536. Before the accuracy of the inscription on the reverse of the painting was discredited, Tietze had already put back the traditional date of 1526 to about 1520; this date is now generally accepted. See also plate 89.

Plate 89
PORTRAIT OF VINCENZO MOSTI, *Florence*. Detail: the head.

Plate 90
VENUS ANADYOMENE. *Canvas, 73.6 × 58.4. Edinburgh, National Gallery of Scotland, loan of the Earl of Ellesmere, 1955.* At one time belonging to the Queen of Sweden, it went from there to the Collection of the Duke of Orléans. X-ray examination shows that formerly the face was in a different position (Kennedy North, 1932). According to Gronau, it is identifiable in the "bath" painted by Titian for the Duke of Ferrara in 1517; Tietze considers it to date from about 1520, which would fit in with the obvious connection between this figure and that of the nude female figure in the Prado *Bacchanal* (plate 81), as Phillips and Pallucchini point out. See also plate 91.

Plate 91
VENUS ANADYOMENE. Detail: the bust.

Plate 92
MADONNA AND CHILD WITH TWO ANGELS. *Fresco (transferred to canvas), 160 × 350. Venice, Ducal Palace.* Vasari mentions it as being by Titian; Ridolfi and Boschini note it as being in the Ducal Palace "at the foot of the staircase that leads from the little Courtyard of the Senators to the end of the loggia on the first floor." Most critics agree with the attribution of the lunette to Titian, but Tietze considers it the work of his school, and Fiocco (1946) sees in it the hand of Francesco Vecellio. Bologna (1951) dates it to about 1510; Fogolari (1935) suggests 1530, and Pallucchini agrees with this while suggesting that it should perhaps be put back to 1523.

Plate 93
MADONNA AND CHILD WITH THREE SAINTS (*Francis, Jerome and Antony Abbot*). *Canvas, 100 × 137. Ansbach, Bayerische Staatsgemäldesammlungen.* Recorded by Ridolfi as being "one of the best works by Titian," this painting was among those sent to Antwerp by Jacopo Casciopino. Cavalcaselle considers it to be by a follower of Titian: namely, Francesco Vecellio; Morelli believes it to be from his workshop with Titian's help; A. Venturi (1954) thinks it definitely to be by Francesco Vecellio. Rightly ascribing the canvas to Titian's youth, Bologna believes he can see in it a collaboration between Titian and Francesco Vecellio.

LOCATION OF PAINTINGS

Portrait of Francesco Maria della Rovere (plate 142).
Portrait of Eleonora Gonzaga della Rovere (plate 143).
The Venus of Urbino (plates 155–156).

GENOA
BALBI DI PIOVERA COLLECTION
Madonna and Child, Two Saints, and a Worshipper (plates 53–54).

GLASGOW
CORPORATION GALLERIES
The Adulteress Before Christ (plates 15–17).

HAMPTON COURT
ROYAL COLLECTION
Portrait of a Man of Letters (plate 87).
Lucretia (plate 114).

INDIANAPOLIS
J. HERRON ART INSTITUTE
Portrait of Ludovico Ariosto (plate 63).

KENOSHA
ALLEN COLLECTION
Portrait of the Doge Andrea Gritti (plate 161a).

KINGSTON LACY
BANKES COLLECTION
Portrait of a Nobleman of the Savorgnan Family (plate 160b).

LENINGRAD
HERMITAGE
Girl with a Feather in Her Hat (plate 141).

LONDON
BATH COLLECTION
Rest on the Flight into Egypt (plate 42).

DEVONSHIRE COLLECTION
Portrait of a Man (plate 86).
HALIFAX COLLECTION
Portrait of a Young Man (plate 62).
NATIONAL GALLERY
Portrait of a Woman: The Serving Woman (plate 33).
Portrait of a Man: Ariosto (plate 34).
"Noli me tangere" (plates 39–40).
The Holy Family and a Shepherd (plate 51).
Bacchus and Ariadne (plates 111–113).
Madonna and Child, with St John and St Catherine (plate 126).
WERNHER COLLECTION
Portrait of Prince Giacoma Doria (plate 160a).

MADRID
PRADO
Madonna and Child, SS Anthony of Padua and Roch (plate 22).
Madonna and Child, and SS Ulfus and Bridget (plate 70).
The Worship of Venus (The Cupids) (plates 78–79).
Bacchanal: The Andrians (plates 80–82).
Portrait of Federico Gonzaga (plates 115–117).
Portrait of Charles V with His Dog (plate 132).
The Address of Alfonso d'Avalos (plate 158).
Portrait of Daniele Barbaro (plate 191).

MILAN
AMBROSIANA
Portrait of an Old Warrior (plate 134).
BRERA
Portrait of Antonio Porcia (plate 146a).
CASTELLO SFORZESCO
Portrait of Signor d'Aramont (plate 165a).

MINNEAPOLIS
INSTITUTE OF ARTS
The Temptation of Christ (plate 185).

MUNICH
BAYERISCHE STAATSGEMÄL-
DESAMMLUNGEN
*Madonna and Child, St John the
Baptist, and the Donor* (plate 49).
Vanity (plate 58).
Portrait of a Man (plate 106).
Formerly in the FLEISCHMANN
GALLERY
Lucretia (plate 1).

NAPLES
NATIONAL GALLERY
CAPODIMONTE
Portrait of Pope Paul III (plates
168–169).

NEW HAVEN
YALE UNIVERSITY ART
GALLERY
The Circumcision (plate 14).

NEW YORK
BENDIT COLLECTION
Portrait of Gabriele Tadino (plate
146b).
DUVEEN COLLECTION
Portrait of a Woman (plate 19).
FRICK COLLECTION
Man in a Red Cap (plate 56).
METROPOLITAN MUSEUM
Madonna and Child (plate 13).
Portrait of a Venetian Nobleman
(plate 32).
SACHS COLLECTION
Bust of a Young Soldier (plate 18).
RABINOWITZ COLLECTION
Portrait of Gerardo Mercatore (plate
164b).

OMAHA
MUSEUM OF FINE ARTS
Man with a Falcon (plate 118a).

OTTAWA
NATIONAL GALLERY OF
CANADA
Portrait of Daniele Barbaro (plate
190).

PADUA
MUSEO CIVICO
The Birth of Adonis (plates 4a
and 5).
The Forest of Polydorus (plates 4b,
6, and 7).
SCUOLA DEL SANTO
St Anthony Healing a Newborn Child
(plates 23–25).
The Jealous Husband (plates 30–31).
The Miracle of the Youth's Leg
(plates 26–29).

PARIS
DE GANAY COLLECTION
Portrait of Alfonso d'Avalos (plate
144).
LOUVRE
Pastoral Concert (plates 20–21).
Young Woman at Her Toilet (plate
59).
Portrait of a Man (plate 107).
The Man with the Glove (plates
108–109).
The Entombment (plate 125).
The Madonna of the Rabbit (plates
127–128).
St Jerome (plate 130).
Allegory of Alfonso d'Avalos (plate
131).
Portrait of Francis I of France
(plate 145).
Christ at Emmaus (plate 147).
The Pardo Venus (plates 153–154).
Christ Crowned with Thorns (plates
170–171).

POMMERSFELDEN
SCHÖNBORN COLLECTION
*Portrait of a Gentleman of the Farnese
Household* (plate 118b).

ROME

BORGHESE GALLERY
Sacred and Profane Love (plates 64–65, 66–69).
CAPITOLINE MUSEUM
The Baptism of Christ (plate 47).
DORIA GALLERY
Salome (plate 61).
SPADA GALLERY
Portrait of a Musician (plate 84).

SÃO PAULO

MUSEU DE ARTE
Portrait of Bishop Cristoforo Madruzzo of Trent (plate 163).

TRAPANI

MUSEO CIVICO
St Francis Receiving the Stigmata (plate 121).

TREVISO

DUOMO
The Annunciation (plates 98–99).
MUSEO CIVICO
Portrait of Sperone Speroni (plate 165b).

URBINO

GALLERIA NAZIONALE DELLE MARCHE
The Resurrection (plate 176).
The Last Supper (plate 177).

VATICAN CITY

VATICAN MUSEUM
Madonna and Child in Glory, with Six Saints (plate 136).
Portrait of the Doge Nicolò Marcello (plate 161b).

VENICE

ACCADEMIA
Presentation of the Virgin in the Temple (plates 148–149, 150–152).
St John the Baptist (plates 172–173).
CHURCH OF SAN GIOVANNI ELEMOSINARIO
St John the Alms-Giver (plates 187–189).

CHURCH OF SAN MARZIALE
Tobias and the Angel (plate 186).
CHURCH OF SANTA MARIA DELLA SALUTE
St Mark Enthroned, with Four Saints (plates 35–37).
The Sacrifice of Isaac (plate 179).
Cain Slaying Abel (plate 180).
David and Goliath (plate 181).
Busts of the Evangelists (plate 182).
Busts of the Fathers of the Church (plate 183).
CHURCH OF SANTA MARIA GLORIOSA DEI FRARI
The Assumption (plates 72–75).
The Pesaro Altarpiece (plates 122–123).
CINI COLLECTION
St George (plate 83).
DUCAL PALACE
Madonna and Child with Two Angels (plate 92).
St Christopher (plate 120).
SCHOOL OF SAN ROCCO
Christ Carrying the Cross with an Executioner (plate 44).
The Annunciation (plate 157).

VERONA

DUOMO
The Assumption of the Virgin (plate 137).

VIENNA

KUNSTHISTORISCHES MUSEUM
The Gypsy Madonna (plate 43).
Tarquin and Lucretia (plate 52).
Portrait of a Young Girl: Violante (plate 55).
The Madonna of the Cherries (plate 77).
Portrait of a Man (plate 85).
The Cut throat (plate 100).
Portrait of Isabella d'Este (plate 139).
Girl in a Fur (plate 140).
"Ecce Homo" (plates 174–175).

REPRODUCTIONS

ACKNOWLEDGMENT FOR
PLATES

Plates 4a and b, 5, 6, 7, 10, 11, 12, 19, 26, 29, 35, 36, 37, 44, 46, 83, 84, 88, 89, 92, 100, 101, 102, 103, 104, 105, 122, 123, 125, 127, 128, 131, 137, 138, 150, 153, 154, 157, 170, 171, 181, 182a, b, c and d, 183a, b, c and d, 186, 187, 188, 189, 201a and b, 202b, 220a: *Fiorentini, Venice.* Plates 8, 9, 22, 45, 47, 51, 61, 64–65, 66, 67, 68, 69, 70, 72, 73, 78, 79, 80, 115, 117, 120, 126, 129, 132, 136, 142, 143, 146a, 151, 152, 155, 156, 158, 161b, 168, 169, 176, 177, 179, 180, 194, 195, 212, 213b: *Anderson, Rome.* Plates 15, 16, 17, 20, 206a: *Ferruzzi, Venice.* Plates 21, 23, 30, 148–149, 162, 172, 197b: *Rossi, Venice.* Plates 24, 25, 27, 28, 31: *A.F.l., Venice.* Plates 41, 59, 60, 74, 75, 98, 99, 107, 108, 109, 133, 134, 145, 147, 192, 193, 223: *Alinari, Florence.* Plates 94, 196, 198b: *Gabinetto Fotografico Nazionale, Rome.* Plates 95, 96, 97, 121: *Istituto Centrale del Restauro, Rome.* Plate 163: *Perotti, Milan.* Plates 173, 217a and b, 218a, b, c and d: *Böhm, Venice.* All other photographs have been provided by the various galleries and collections concerned. Material for Color plates I and II was supplied by the National Gallery, London, and for plates III and IV by *Scala, Florence.*

Plate I. LUCRETIA
formerly in Munich, Fleischmann Gallery

Plate 2. PORTRAIT OF A MAN
Washington, National Gallery of Art, Kress Collection

Plate 3. *Detail of plate 2*

Plate 4. THE BIRTH OF ADONIS, *and*
THE FOREST OF POLYDORUS
Padua, Museo Civico

Plate 5. *Detail of plate 4a*

Plate 6. *Detail of plate 4b*

Plate 7. *Detail of plate 4b*

Plate 8. ORPHEUS AND EURYDICE
Bergamo, Accademia Carrara, Lochis Collection

Plate 9. *Detail of plate 8*

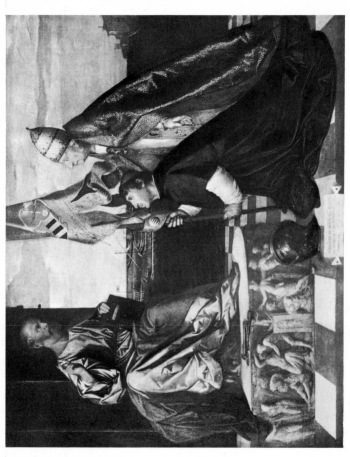

Plate 10. ST PETER, POPE ALEXANDER VI, AND BISHOP PESARO
Antwerp, Musée Royal des Beaux-Arts

Plate 11. *Detail of plate 10*

Plate 12. *Detail of plate 10*

Plate 13. MADONNA AND CHILD
New York, Metropolitan Museum, J. S. Bache Collection

Plate 14. THE CIRCUMCISION
New Haven, Yale University Art Gallery

Plate 15. THE ADULTERESS BEFORE CHRIST
Glasgow, Corporation Galleries

Plate 16. *Detail of plate 15*

Plate 17. *Detail of plate 15*

Plate 18. BUST OF A YOUNG SOLDIER
New York, Sachs Collection

Plate 19. PORTRAIT OF A WOMAN
New York, Duveen Brothers Collection

Plate 20. PASTORAL CONCERT
Paris, Louvre

Plate 21. *Detail of plate 20*

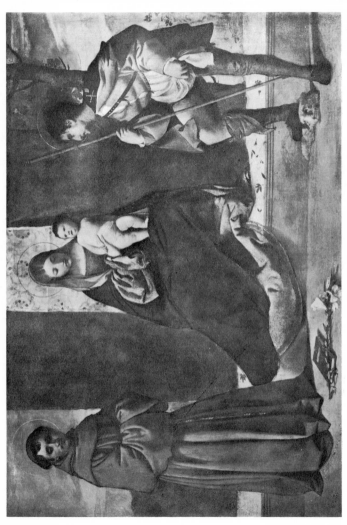

Plate 22. MADONNA AND CHILD WITH SS ANTHONY OF PADUA AND
ROCH, Madrid, Prado

Plate 23. ST ANTHONY HEALING A NEWBORN CHILD
Padua, Scuola del Santo

Plate 24. *Detail of plate 23*

Plate 25. *Detail of plate 23*

Plate 26. THE MIRACLE OF THE YOUTH'S LEG
Padua, Scuola del Santo

Plate 27. *Detail of plate 26*

Plate 28. *Detail of plate 26*

Plate 29. *Detail of plate 26*

Plate 30. THE JEALOUS HUSBAND
Padua, Scuola del Santo

Plate 31. *Detail of plate 30*

Plate 32. PORTRAIT OF A MAN
New York, Metropolitan Museum

PORTRAIT OF A MAN (ARIOSTO)
London, National Gallery
(detail of plate 34)

Plate 33. PORTRAIT OF A WOMAN (THE SERVING WOMAN)
London, National Gallery

Plate 34. PORTRAIT OF A MAN (ARIOSTO)
London, National Gallery

Plate 35. ST MARK ENTHRONED WITH FOUR SAINTS
Venice, Church of Santa Maria della Salute. Sacristy

Plate 36. *Detail of plate 35*

Plate 37. *Detail of plate 35*

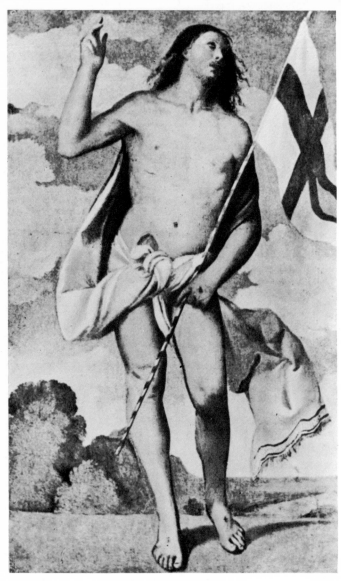

Plate 38. THE RISEN CHRIST
formerly in Milan. Achillito Chiesa Collection

Plate 39. "NOLI ME TANGERE"
London, National Gallery

Plate 40. *Detail of plate 39*

"NOLI ME TANGERE"
London, National Gallery
(*detail of plate 39*)

Plate 41. LANDSCAPE OF THE "SLEEPING VENUS" BY GIORGIONE
Dresden, Gemäldegalerie

Plate 42. REST ON THE FLIGHT INTO EGYPT
London, Marquess of Bath Collection

Plate 43. THE GYPSY MADONNA
Vienna, Kunsthistorisches Museum

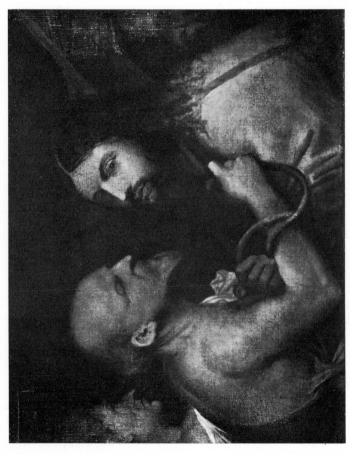

Plate 44. CHRIST CARRYING THE CROSS WITH AN EXECUTIONER
Venice, School of San Rocco

Plate 45. CONCERT
Florence, Pitti Palace

Plate 46. *Detail of plate 45*

Plate 47. THE BAPTISM OF CHRIST
Rome, Capitoline Museum

Plate 48. THE THREE AGES OF LIFE
Edinburgh, National Gallery of Scotland, loan of the Earl of Ellesmere (1955)

Plate 49. MADONNA AND CHILD, ST JOHN THE BAPTIST, AND THE
DONOR, Munich, Bayerische Staatsgemäldesammlungen

Plate 50. MADONNA AND CHILD, ST JOHN THE BAPTIST, AND THE DONOR. Edinburgh, National Gallery of Scotland, loan of the Earl of Ellesmere

Plate 51. THE HOLY FAMILY AND A SHEPHERD
London, National Gallery

Plate 52. TARQUIN AND LUCRETIA
Vienna, Kunsthistorisches Museum

Plate 53. MADONNA AND CHILD, TWO SAINTS, AND A WORSHIPPER
Genoa, Collection of Marchese Balbi di Piovera

Plate 54. *Detail of plate 53*

Plate 55. PORTRAIT OF A YOUNG GIRL (VIOLANTE)
Vienna, Kunsthistorisches Museum

Plate 56. MAN IN A RED CAP
New York, Frick Collection

CONCERT
Florence, Pitti Palace
(detail of plate 45)

Plate 57. PORTRAIT OF A MAN
Copenhagen, Statens Museum for Kunst

Plate 58. VANITY
Munich, Bayerische Staatsgemäldesammlungen

Plate 59. YOUNG WOMAN AT HER TOILET
Paris, Louvre

Plate 60. FLORA
Florence, Uffizi

Plate 61. SALOME
Rome, Doria Gallery

Plate 62. PORTRAIT OF A YOUNG MAN
London, Collection of the Earl of Halifax

Plate 63. PORTRAIT OF LUDOVICO ARIOSTO
Indianapolis, J. Herron Art Institute

Plates 64–65. SACR
Rome, B

ND PROFANE LOVE
se Gallery

Plate 66. *Detail of plates 64–65*

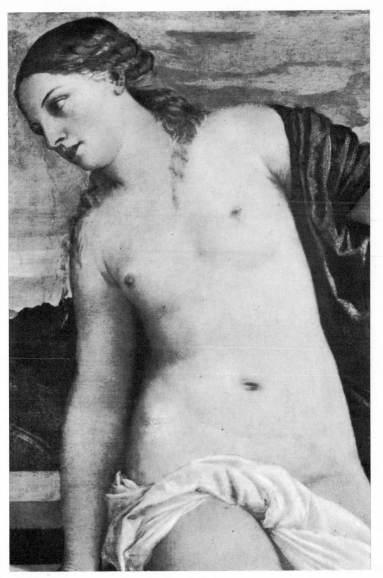

Plate 67. *Detail of plates 64–65*

Plate 68. *Detail of plates 64–65*

Plate 69. *Detail of plates 64–65*

Plate 70. MADONNA AND CHILD, AND SS ULFUS AND BRIDGET
Madrid, Prado

Plate 71. SACRED CONVERSATION
Dresden, Gemäldegalerie

Plate 72. THE ASSUMPTION OF THE VIRGIN
Venice, Church of Santa Maria Gloriosa dei Frari

SACRED AND PROFANE LOVE
Rome, Borghese Gallery
(*detail of plates 64–65*)

Plate 73. *Detail of plate 72*

Plate 74. *Detail of plate 72*

Plate 75. *Detail of plate 72*

Plate 76. THE TRIBUTE MONEY
Dresden, Gemäldegalerie

Plate 77. THE MADONNA OF THE CHERRIES
Vienna, Kunsthistorisches Museum

Plate 78. THE WORSHIP OF VENUS
Madrid, Prado

Plate 79. *Detail of plate 78*

Plate 80. BACCHANAL (THE ANDRIANS)
Madrid, Prado

Plate 81. *Detail of plate 80*

Plate 82. *Detail of plate 80*

Plate 83. ST GEORGE
Venice, Cini Collection

Plate 84. PORTRAIT OF A MUSICIAN
Rome, Spada Gallery

Plate 85. PORTRAIT OF A MAN
Vienna, Kunsthistorisches Museum

Plate 86. PORTRAIT OF A MAN
London, Collection of the Duke of Devonshire

Plate 87. PORTRAIT OF A MAN OF LETTERS
Hampton Court, Royal Collection

Plate 88. PORTRAIT OF VINCENZO MOSTI
Florence, Pitti Palace

Plate 89. *Detail of plate 88*

Plate 90. VENUS ANADYOMENE
Edinburgh, National Gallery of Scotland, loan of the Earl of Ellesmere (1955)

Plate 91. *Detail of plate 90*

Plate 92. MADONNA AND CHILD, WITH TWO ANGELS
Venice, Ducal Palace

Plate 93. MADONNA AND CHILD WITH THREE SAINTS
Ansbach, Bayerische Staatsgemäldesammlungen